Eyes Open 3 — Combo A
STUDENT'S BOOK with Digital Pack

Ben Goldstein & **Ceri Jones**
with **Eoin Higgins**

Starter Unit	Vocabulary		Language focus	
	p4 Meeting people, routines, free-time activities **p5** Adjectives, adverbs		**p4** *Wh-* questions, comparative and superlative adjectives **p6** Comparative and superlative adverbs, past simple **p98** Grammar reference	

Unit	Vocabulary	Reading	Language focus 1	Listening and vocabulary
1 **Extreme living**	**p9** Extreme weather **p96 Say it right!** /ɪ/ and /iː/	**p10** A blog **Explore** words in context	**p11** Present simple vs. present continuous ▶ The long winter	**p12** A conversation Survival essentials
2 **A balancing act**	**p19** Priorities	**p20** A magazine article **Explore** verb + noun collocations	**p21** *should/must* ▶ Get up and go!	**p22** A radio interview Performing **p96 Say it right!** Word stress
	Review Unit 1 and 2 page 28–29			
3 Art all around us	**p31** Art around us **Get it right!** *go there*	**p32** An online debate **Explore** collocations	**p33** Present perfect for indefinite past time **Get it right!** *gone* and *been* ▶ The art of storytelling	**p34** An interview Musical instruments
4 Adventure	**p41** Expressions with *go*	**p42** An online advertisement **Explore** words in context	**p43** Present perfect with *still, yet, already* and *just* ▶ The age of discovery	**p44** An interview Phrasal verbs **p96 Say it right!** Consonant to vowel linking
	Review Unit 3 and 4 page 50–51			

Projects p123–124   Irregular verbs and phonemic script: back of book

Speaking and listening

p4 Meeting people
p7 ▶ **Real talk:** Do you often lose things?, explaining a problem

Language focus 2	Discover Culture (Video and Reading)	Speaking	Writing	Extras
p13 Past simple vs. past continuous	**p14** ▶ People of the mangrove jungle **p15** A magazine article **Explore** prepositional phrases	**p16** ▶ **Real talk:** Which do you prefer – towns and cities or the countryside? Giving your opinion	**p17** An email to a friend **Useful language:** Opening and closing an email	**p115 CLIL** Biology – Global warming ▶ Hot topics **p99 Grammar reference** **p107 Vocabulary bank**
p23 *(don't) have to/ mustn't*	**p24** ▶ A life on Broadway **p25** An article **Explore** prepositions	**p26** ▶ **Real talk:** What makes a good friend? Offering to help	**p27** A competition entry **Useful language:** Avoiding repetition (1)	**p116 CLIL** P.E. – Avoiding sports injuries ▶ Mountain rescue **p100 Grammar reference** **p108 Vocabulary bank**
p35 Present perfect with *ever/never* **p96 Say it right!** Strong and weak forms	**p36** ▶ A world of music **p37** A web page **Explore** phrasal verbs with *up*	**p38** ▶ **Real talk:** Have you ever been to a concert? Invitations and arrangements	**p39** An internet post **Useful language:** Avoiding repetition (2)	**p117 CLIL** Art – Perspective ▶ Art in perspective **p101 Grammar reference** **p109 Vocabulary bank**
p45 Present perfect with *for* or *since* Present perfect and past simple	**p46** ▶ The strange and beautiful land of Australia **p47** A poster presentation **Explore** interesting adjectives	**p48** ▶ **Real talk:** What's the most exciting thing you've ever done? Signing up for an activity	**p49** A travel blog **Useful language:** Expressing how you feel, good or bad	**p118 CLIL** Geography – Time zones ▶ Where in the world? **p102 Grammar reference** **p110 Vocabulary bank**

Starter Unit

Meeting people

1 🔊 **1.01** Complete the conversation with the words in the box. Then listen, check and repeat.

> See   I'm   This   Goodbye   ~~My~~
> your   is   Pleased   Her   from

Kieran: Hello. ¹*My* name's Kieran. What's ²…. name?
Fay: Hi, Kieran. I'm Fay. ³…. is my friend. ⁴…. name's Gulay.
Gulay: ⁵…. to meet you Kieran!
Kieran: Where are you ⁶…., Gulay?
Gulay: ⁷…. from Istanbul in Turkey.
Fay: Gulay ⁸…. staying at our house.
Kieran: Well, I have to go. ⁹…. you later!
Fay: ¹⁰…. Kieran!

Routines

2 Match the daily routines with the pictures.

> have lunch   ~~wake up~~   get up   have dinner
> have breakfast   go to bed   have a shower
> do homework   go to school

a   *wake up*

3 Work with a partner. Use the activities in Exercise 2 to describe a typical day in your life.

I wake up at 7.30 am and I get up quickly. Then I have a shower and have breakfast at 8 am.

Free-time activities

4 Complete the free-time activities with *do*, *go*, *play*, *read*, *sing* or *watch*.

1 *go* cycling
2 … judo
3 … football
4 … a book
5 … swimming
6 … exercise
7 … the guitar
8 … a song
9 … basketball
10 … a film

5 Ask and answer questions about the activities in Exercise 5 with your partner.

A: *Do you go cycling at weekends?*
B: *No, I haven't got a bicycle!*

Wh- questions

6 Match the questions and the answers.

1 Where do you live?
2 How old is this car?
3 How are you today?
4 Whose birthday is it tomorrow?
5 When did you go to London?
6 What are you doing?

a I'm fine, thanks. And you?
b I'm waiting for the bus.
c It's three years old.
d We went last summer.
e It's Cristina's. She's 14.
f In Paris.

7 Write the words in order to make questions.

1 study / you / Where / do ?
2 old / you / are / How ?
3 like / do / TV programmes / What / watching / you ?
4 on holiday / you / Where / next summer / go / will ?
5 teacher / last year / Who / English / your / was ?
6 get / this morning / How / you / to school / did ?

8 Ask and answer the questions in Exercise 7 with your partner.

Adjectives

1 Choose the correct words to complete the sentences.
1. My brother is so (annoying) / friendly / weird – he is always borrowing my things.
2. Frank plays the guitar – he's really **excited / interested / surprised** in music.
3. My favourite comedian is Will Ferrell – he is so **funny / moody / unfriendly**!
4. I get really **embarrassed / interested / bored** when the news comes on – I change the channel.
5. I think Sam is a bit **tired / angry / upset** after the long journey so he's not coming out tonight.
6. I find films with clowns really **cheerful / scary / impatient**. I have nightmares after watching them.

2 Work with a partner. Use the adjectives in Exercise 1 to describe the following people.
1. a friend
2. a relative (brother, sister, uncle, aunt, etc.)
3. a teacher at school
4. a famous person

My friend Gill is really impatient; she hates waiting for the bus! She's really interested in cooking.

Comparative and superlative adjectives

3 🔊 **1.02** Complete the conversations about TV programmes with the comparative or superlative adjectives. Then listen and check.
1. **A:** I think documentaries are .... (interesting) the news.
   B: Really? I don't like documentaries or the news. Cartoons are the .... (good) thing on TV, in my opinion!
2. **A:** I think the .... (boring) programmes on TV are chat shows – I hate them!
   B: Yes, I know what you mean. But I think reality shows are the .... (bad)!
3. **A:** I love watching romantic films! It's much .... (relaxing) watching action films!
   B: Oh no, I love action films. They are .... (exciting) romantic films and they have the .... (good) special effects!

4 Work with a partner. Use comparatives and superlatives to compare TV shows you know.

Adverbs

5 Choose the correct words to complete the sentences.
1. Tina and I spoke **quiet / (quietly)** because Niall was studying.
2. We were all **happy / happily** to see Vicky again.
3. I'm sorry. I draw very **bad / badly**. What do you think?
4. We ran **quick / quickly** but the bus left without us.
5. Everyone thought it was an **easy / easily** exam.
6. Ian speaks French very **good / well**. He lived there for a year.
7. Drive **slow / slowly** Granny. I think Susan's house is near here.
8. Be **careful / carefully** – they bite!

6 Match four of the sentences in Exercise 5 to the pictures below.

Comparative and superlative adverbs

1 David is writing about his classmates. Complete the text with the comparative and superlative adverbs of the adjectives in brackets.

So these are my classmates – we're all really different. Alice is the best in the class. She works ¹ _more quickly_ (quick) than anyone else in the class. Ryan is good at Maths so he does his Maths homework ² …. (easy). Christine does her homework ³ …. (careful) than anyone else but it takes her hours so she definitely does things ⁴ …. (slow). I sit beside Paola. I can draw ⁵ …. (good) than she can but she's really nice and she sits ⁶ …. (quiet) than I do.

Past simple

2 Complete the table with the past simple form of the verbs in the box.

| ~~watch~~ ~~leave~~ help dance get go be wash |
| come walk stop take eat work have see |

Regular	Irregular
watched	left

3 Complete the sentences with the past simple form of the regular verbs in Exercise 2.

1 It was a lovely day so we _walked_ around the park.
2 My mum …. in a cinema when she was young.
3 Tell me about the film. I …. (not) it last night because I went to bed early.
4 …. you …. Carl with his homework?
5 It was a great party and the music was amazing. We …. for hours.
6 Sorry we're late. We …. at a shop to buy some ice cream.
7 I …. my dad's car two hours ago and now it's raining!

4 Complete the news story with the past simple form of the irregular verbs in Exercise 2. Use one verb twice.

Last weekend, my family and I ¹ _went_ to the mountains. It ² …. great. We ³ …. a really good time. We ⁴ …. early in the morning. My cousin Gina ⁵ …. with us. We ⁶ …. some food – sandwiches and drinks – and we ⁷ …. under the trees in the forest. We ⁸ …. some beautiful birds. When we ⁹ …. home we ¹⁰ …. very tired but happy.

5 Write three true past simple sentences about you, your friends or your family with the verbs and the time expressions.

eat	ago
see	last week
watch	yesterday
be	last weekend
walk	last month
had	last Friday
come	yesterday morning
wash	last year
dance	

My friend Anne ate pizza last Friday.

Speaking Explaining a problem

Real talk: Do you often lose things?

1 ▶ 0.1 Watch the teenagers in the video. How many teens lost something once?

2 💬 Do *you* often lose things?

3 🔊 1.03 Shelley and Ed are talking about a problem. What did Shelley lose?

4 Complete the conversation with the useful language.

Useful language

I don't know what to do.
What's the matter?
I'm not sure.
OK, don't panic!
Oh no!
For one thing (no one rang me).
Let me think …
I hope so!

5 🔊 1.03 Listen again and check your answers.

6 💬 Work with a partner. Practise the conversation in Exercise 4.

7 💬 Change the words in bold in the dialogue. Use the ideas below. Take turns to talk to a friend and explain what the problem is. Use the situations below or your own ideas.

Problem 1

You are at school. Your mobile isn't in your bag. It's new and was quite expensive. It has all your numbers in it and hundreds of songs. You had it this morning at home.

Problem 2

You are at a friend's house. You can't find your memory stick. It has all the work you did for a group presentation. You need it tomorrow. You had it earlier today at school.

Ed:	Hi, Shelley! What's the ¹ *matter* ?
Shelley:	I can't find **my school bag**! It's got **all my books** in!
Ed:	Oh ² …. ! Where did you go **after school**?
Shelley:	Umm, let me ³ …. . I went to **watch a basketball match**. After that, I **went to buy a drink**, and then we **went to the park**.
Ed:	Did you leave it **in the park**?
Shelley:	I'm ⁴ …. . I was **on my way home** when I realised I didn't have it. I went back **to the park** but I couldn't find it! I don't ⁵ …. to do!
Ed:	OK, don't ⁶ …. . Perhaps **a friend** saw it and took it **home**.
Shelley:	No, I don't think so. For one ⁷ …. , no one rang me.
Ed:	Well, maybe you left it **in the shop**. Let's go and ask if it's there.
Shelley:	OK – I ⁸ …. !

1 Extreme living

In this unit …

The long winter p11

People of the mangrove jungle p14

Giving your opinion p16

CLIL Hot topics p115

Vocabulary
- Extreme weather
- Words from the text
- Survival essentials
- Prepositional phrases

Language focus
- Present simple and present continuous
- Past simple and past continuous

Unit aims
I can …
- understand a blog about extreme weather.
- describe where I live and past activities.
- understand a conversation about a news story.
- understand an article about a remote island.
- give my opinion, agree and disagree politely.
- write an email to a penfriend.

BE CURIOUS
What can you see in the photo?
Start thinking
- What do you think the man is doing?
- What is it like to live in a country with very cold weather?
- How do you think people keep warm in cold countries?

Vocabulary Extreme weather

1 🔊 1.04 Match the words and phrases in the box with the pictures (a–h). Then listen, check and repeat.

> hail boiling freezing heavy rain heatwave
> thunder and lightning snowstorm high winds

a *boiling*

2 What months of the year do you think about with the weather words in Exercise 3?

In July, it is usually boiling but in October we have heavy rain.

3 🔊 1.05 Listen to the radio show. Write the weather words from Exercise 3.
1 Victor (Argentina)   *heatwave, boiling*   3 Oksana (Russia)
2 Hannah (England)   4 Silke (Germany)

➜ Say it right! • page 96

Your turn

4 Make notes about extreme weather conditions in your country.

5 Work with a partner. What does he/she do in extreme weather? Then report your partner's answers to the class.

A: What do you do when it's freezing?
B: I wear a lot of clothes and a scarf, hat and gloves.

➜ Vocabulary Bank • page 107

Reading A blog

1 Work with a partner. Look at the photos and answer the questions.
1. Where is Yakutsk, do you think?
2. What is special about it?

2 🔊 1.09 Meg is a British student at the University of Yakutsk in Siberia, Russia. Read her blog. Do you think she prefers summer or winter there?

3 Read Meg's blog again. Answer the questions.
1. What is Meg doing now? *Meg is sitting indoors and writing her blog.*
2. What is the average daytime temperature in Yakutsk in winter?
3. What effect does the extreme cold have on people's bodies?
4. Why is she learning how to play kyyly?
5. How many hours of sunlight do they get in Yakutsk in summer?
6. What do people do in the summer in Yakutsk?

Explore words in context

4 Match the words and phrases from the blog with the definitions below.

> fall   outdoors   indoors   sub-zero conditions   melt   rise

1. inside a house or building
2. outside a house or building
3. get lower
4. change from solid to liquid
5. get higher
6. when the temperature is less than 0 °C

Your turn

5 Ask and answer with your partner.
1. How is life in your town different in summer and in winter? In what way?
2. Do you prefer winter or summer? Why?

> In the summer, it's very hot. I prefer the winter because …

6 Write a short blog entry.
- Describe the weather in winter and summer in your area.
- Say what you're doing now.

In the winter, it's really cold. The temperatures are below freezing and it snows a lot.
At the moment, I'm writing this blog and I'm watching …

FREEZING IN SIBERIA!

December 12

It's winter here in Yakutsk. I'm sitting indoors and writing my blog because it's too cold to go outside. It's not snowing now but I'm looking at the thermometer outside and it says –34 °C!

Yakutsk in Russia is the coldest town on Earth. From November to March, it's only light for three or four hours a day and the temperature hardly ever rises above freezing. The average daytime temperature is –30 °C and at night it sometimes falls as low as –60 °C.

Well, I'm not going out today – I'm staying indoors. People don't go out a lot here, at –20 °C, the air freezes inside your nose. At –40 °C, you can't stay outdoors for more than ten minutes. At –45 °C, the metal on your glasses sticks to your face! I'm learning how to play a popular sport called kyyly – a kind of jumping competition. It uses a lot of energy and it keeps you warm and strong. I play kyyly three times a week. I'm trying to keep fit, which is really important when you live in sub-zero conditions!

In summer, Yakutsk is a different city. The snow melts and the temperature rises to 30 °C and more, but people are usually happy to have a heatwave after ten months of winter. It's the season of 'white nights', when it never gets dark, not even at midnight. Camping and barbecues are the favourite summer activities. You can't imagine how much I am looking forward to it!

FACT! In Yakutsk, Siberia, the lowest ever recorded temperature was –60 °C.

Language focus 1 Present simple vs. present continuous

1 **Complete the examples from the text on page 10. Then complete the rules in the box.**
   1 It's .... now but **I'm looking** at the thermometer outside and **it says** –34 °C!
   2 I .... how to play a popular local sport called kyyly. It .... a lot of energy.

> We use the present [1] .... to talk about what normally happens, routines and facts. We use the present [2] .... to talk about what is happening now or around now.

   3 The temperature .... rises above freezing.
   4 It .... falls as low as –60 °C.
   5 People are .... happy to have a heatwave after ten months of winter.

> We use adverbs and expressions of frequency to explain how often we do things. We use them with the [3] .... . Adverbs of frequency go before the verb but after the verb *be*.

➜ **Grammar reference • page 99**

2 🔊 1.10 **Complete the text with the correct form of the present simple or the present continuous. Use the verbs in brackets. Then listen and check.**

Meg is in Siberia for a year at the university in Yakutsk and life is very different. In the UK, she usually [1] ....*drives*.... (drive) to university. In Yakutsk, she [2] .... (take) the bus every day. She [3] .... (study) Russian in the UK and she'd like to be a translator. She's got exams this week so she [4] .... (study) really hard. She says, 'Right now I [5] .... (read) a book in Russian. I [6] .... (try) not to use the dictionary too much.' She [7] .... (have) a great time in Yakutsk because she [8] .... (go) to the university International Club twice a week. They [9] .... (organise) activities and she meets lots of local students there. 'It's great fun. The people are really nice and I [10] .... (learn) a lot of Russian.'

3 **Add expressions of frequency to make sentences that are true for you.**
   1 It's very cold in my town. *It's usually very cold in my town.*
   2 I get to school late.
   3 My class goes on school trips in June.
   4 It's sunny and warm in spring.
   5 We go camping.

Your turn

4 **Work with a partner. Discuss the sentences.**
   1 Tell your partner about your daily routine.
   2 Imagine you're staying in Yakutsk for a month. Tell your partner about how your life is different.

> I usually get up at about 7.30. Then I have breakfast. ... Now I'm living in Yakutsk, I get up later …

Learn about someone living in a cold country.
- What does the Kilcher family do during the day?
- What are they preparing for?
- Why did they have to make another plan?

Discovery EDUCATION
1.1 The long winter

Vocabulary Survival essentials

1 🔊 1.11 Match the words with the items in the picture. Then listen, check and repeat.

> sun cream   water bottle   sunglasses   compass
> map   sleeping bag   penknife   torch
> first aid kit   camera   glasses   contact lenses

2 Ask and answer with your partner.
1. Which of the things in Exercise 1 do you have on your mobile phone?
2. Which of the things do you have at home?

➡ **Vocabulary Bank • page 107**

Listening A conversation

3 Work in small groups. Look at the photo and answer the questions.
1. What do you think are the dangers of walking in a landscape like this?
2. What do you need to survive for three days there?

4 🔊 1.12 Listen to two friends discussing a news story about a hiker. Does it have a happy or sad ending?

5 🔊 1.12 Listen again and answer the questions.
1. In which country was Sam travelling?
2. What happened to him?
3. What was the weather like?
4. How long was he lost for?
5. What objects did Sam have with him?
6. How did the contact lenses save him?
7. How did they find him in the end?

> **Your turn**

6 Imagine you are lost in the mountains in the winter. With a partner decide how important the things in Exercise 1 are.
- Put them in order of importance (1 = very important; 12 = not important).
- Compare your list with another pair.
- Think of three other things that are useful.

A: I think … is/are important because …
B: I don't agree. I think …

Language focus 2 Past simple vs. past continuous

1 Complete the examples from the listening on page 12. Then complete the rules and choose the correct words in the box.

1. One morning he **went** jogging.
2. While he .... **jogging** he got lost.
3. He .... **running** and **listening** to music.
4. He .... **see** where he was going.
5. How long .... he **lost** for?
6. .... someone **looking** for him?

> We use the past ¹.... to talk about finished actions in the past. We use the past ².... to talk about actions in progress in the past.
> ³ We use *when / while* before the past simple.
> ⁴ We use *when / while* before the past continuous.

➡ **Grammar reference** • page 99

2 Choose the correct verbs to complete the sentences.
1. Sam **jogged** / **was jogging** when he **got** / **was getting** lost.
2. I **watched** / **was watching** the news when I **saw** / **was seeing** an interesting story.
3. When the helicopter **found** / **was finding** him, a lot of people **looked** / **were looking** for him.
4. When he **ran** / **was running** out of water, he **still tried** / **was still trying** to find the ranch.
5. It **didn't rain** / **wasn't raining** when Sam **started** / **was starting** his run.
6. He **lost** / **was losing** his sunglasses while he **walked** / **was walking** in the outback.

3 Rewrite the sentences in two different ways. Use *when* or *while*.
1. Peter was walking in the forest. He got lost.
   While Peter was walking in the forest, he got lost.
   Peter was walking in the forest when he got lost.
2. We were driving. A dog ran in front of our car.
3. She was looking at the map. She dropped her camera.
4. I was reading the compass. Julia was putting on suncream.
5. We were sleeping in our tent. It started to rain.

4 🔊 **1.13** Complete the text with the correct form of the verbs in brackets. Then listen and check.

TEENAGERS IN CANYON RESCUE

Emergency services ¹ *rescued* (rescue) two teenagers, Nicholas Ramirez and Kyndall Cendoya, last night after a three-day hunt in Falls Canyon, California. The teenagers ² .... (walk) during the Easter holidays when they ³ .... (disappear) late on Tuesday night. It ⁴ .... (rain) heavily and there were high winds. The teenagers ⁵ .... (not have) any food or water and they ⁶ .... (not carry) any dry clothes in their backpacks. They ⁷ .... (find) a cave and ⁸ .... (stay) there for two nights. On the third day, a local hiker ⁹ .... (see) them. They ¹⁰ .... (sleep) in the cave. A rescue helicopter ¹¹ .... (come) to take them home.

Your turn

5 Write six questions. Use the words from the boxes and the past simple or past continuous.

what when where why	do come sleep watch go eat listen	last night morning yesterday at 8am during the English class

Why were you sleeping during the English class?

6 Ask and answer with your partner.

A: *What were you doing yesterday at 8 am?*
B: *I was watching TV.*

Discover Culture

1 Work with a partner. Look at the photo of the mangrove jungle. How do you think it is different from a normal jungle?

2 In which one do you think it would be easier to live? Why? Consider transport, food and climate.

A mangrove jungle

A jungle

Find out about the challenges of living in the mangrove jungle.

1.2 People of the mangrove jungle

3 ▶ 1.2 Watch the first half of the video (until 1.00). Mark the sentences true (T) or false (F).
   1 In India, the River Ganges runs into the sea.
   2 There are 1,000 islands in the Sunderbans.
   3 One of these islands is called Bali.
   4 Life is quite easy there.
   5 The people live off rice, fish and potatoes.

4 ▶ 1.2 Watch the second half of the video. Put this information into the correct order.
   a They decided to build a high wall to protect their homes.
   b They ate the fish.
   c They saw the sea level rise.
   d They noticed a break in the wall.
   e They worked for three hours to fix the break.
   f They caught a lot of fish.
   g They remembered that their village flooded years ago.

5 ▶ 1.2 Watch the video again. Read Exercises 1 and 2 again. Are your answers the same now? How do the images show the positive and negative side of life in the Mangrove Jungle?

6 Test your memory. These sentences describe different images in the video but each one has a mistake. Correct the false information.
   1 There are dry rice fields.
   2 There are four men on the boat.
   3 We see a half moon.
   4 There's a man carrying a lantern on his head.

7 ▶ 1.2 Watch the video again and check your answers.

8 What is life like in the Indian Mangroves? Choose the best summary.
   1 Life is okay in the mangroves if you are careful.
   2 Life is very hard in the mangroves.
   3 Life is easy and relaxed in the mangroves.

Your turn

9 Work with a partner. Is there any part of your country like the Mangroves? Is there an area surrounded by a lot of water? Would you like to live there? Why?/Why not?

There are lots of towns on the river and they are sometimes flooded, so I wouldn't like to live there.

Reading A magazine article

1. **Work with a partner. Look at the photo and answer the questions.**
   1. Where do you think this place is?
   2. What do you think is special about it?

2. 🔊 **1.14 Read the article and check your answers.**

3. **Read the article again and complete the information.**
   Approximate distance from the mainland: *4,000 km*
   Official language:
   Approximate distance from London:
   Number of families:
   Length of island:
   Number of schools:
   Month and year that the volcano erupted:

Explore prepositional phrases

4. **Find the phrases in the article and complete them using *in* or *on*.**
   1. *On* Earth
   2. …. the middle
   3. …. the planet
   4. …. a ship
   5. …. total
   6. …. the island

   ➡ **Vocabulary Bank • page 107**

Your turn

5. **Work with a partner. Compare the life on islands like Bali and Tristan de Cunha. How are they similar?**

   > They are both islands and they are small communities.

   > Something bad happened on both islands – the volcano erupted on Tristan and there was flooding on Bali.

THE REMOTEST INHABITED ISLAND ON EARTH!

In the middle of the Atlantic Ocean, more than 4,000 km from the nearest land, is the remotest inhabited island on the planet – it is also a volcanic island. To get there, you need to travel for five or six days on a ship from Cape Town in South Africa.

Tristan da Cunha is a British territory, named after the Portuguese explorer who discovered the island. The official language is English, but London is almost 10,000 km away. The British monarch is the head of state and they use British pounds as their currency.

The island is home to eighty families, about 250 people in total. The island is only 10 km long and there is one town with only one school. This is the only place on the island with an internet connection.

In October 1961, the island's volcano erupted and the whole population went to live in the UK. They got jobs and new homes, but they didn't like the lifestyle there and missed their life on the island. They found it very hard to live in a society where money is the most important thing. So, in November 1962, they returned to Tristan da Cunha – they were happier without television, cars and the stress of modern life!

> **FACT!** Queen Mary Peak, the volcano in the middle of the island, is 2000 metres high – and it's active!

Speaking Giving your opinion

Real talk: Which do you prefer – towns and cities or the countryside?

1 ▶ **1.3** Watch the teenagers in the video. How many of them …
   a) like the countryside?
   b) like towns or cities?
   c) like both?

2 Which do *you* prefer – towns and cities or the countryside? Ask and answer with your partner.

3 🔊 **1.15** Listen to Mark and Kate talking about their town. What places do they talk about?

4 Complete the conversation with the useful language.

> ### Useful language
>
> I (don't) think (so) …   Yes, I suppose so.
> Maybe, but …   OK, perhaps you're
> I reckon …   right, …
> I (don't) agree …

Kate:	Do you live near the school, Mark?
Mark:	No, I live in Chesterton. Do you know it?
Kate:	Yes, I live there too. I ¹......*think*...... it's a great place to live.
Mark:	²… so! Nothing ever happens, and there's nothing to do. It's boring.
Kate:	Well, I don't ³… . There are lots of things to do. What about the sports centre and the youth club?
Mark:	Maybe, ⁴… all my friends live here in town, and I can't go out with them in the evening.
Kate:	OK, ⁵… right – that is a problem, but I ⁶… Chesterton is healthier than town.
Mark:	The air you mean? Yes, ⁷… so. I like taking my dog for walks in the country.
Kate:	You see? Maybe living in a village isn't all bad.
Mark:	OK, perhaps you're ⁸… !

5 🔊 **1.15** Listen again and check your answers.

6 Work with a partner. Practise the conversation in Exercise 4.

7 Work with a partner. Prepare a conversation like the one in Exercise 4. Use the photos below and the useful language. Practise the conversation with your partner.

A Living in a city

B Going to a big school

Writing An email to a friend

1 Look at the photos and read Artur's email to a pen friend. Where does Artur live?

> Hi,
>
> Thanks for your email. It's great to hear from you!
>
> I live in a small town in the north of Norway, called Tromsø. It's a special place because in summer we have 60 polar days. It never gets dark and we have the midnight sun. I love the summer!
>
> We do a lot of outdoor activities like trekking in the mountains, bike riding, concerts, boating, barbeques on the beach and sunbathing. We need the sun because in the winter we have 60 polar nights when it's always dark! In winter, tourists come here to see the famous northern lights (the aurora borealis). They are amazing!
>
> Where do you live? What do you do there?
>
> Write back soon,
>
> Best wishes,
>
> Artur

2 Read Artur's email again. Put the information in the correct order.
- closing the email
- a description of his town
- questions to his friend
- opening the email *1*
- activities he does at different times of the year

Useful language

We use special phrases to open and close an email to a friend:
- Opening an email: *Thanks for your email.* …. , …. , ….
- Closing an email: *Write back soon, Best wishes,* …. , ….

3 Look at the Useful language box. Add the examples below to it.

> How are you (and your family)?
> Thanks for all your news.
> Write back and tell me your news.
> It was great to get your email.
> Hope to hear from you soon.

Get Writing

PLAN

4 Plan an email to Artur describing where you live. Use Exercise 2 to help you and make notes.

WRITE

5 Write your email. Use your notes from Exercise 4 and the model text to help you.

CHECK

6 Can you say YES to these questions?
- Is the information from Exercise 4 in your email?
- Have you got opening and closing phrases in your email?

2 A balancing act

In this unit ...

Get up and go! p21

A life on Broadway p24

What makes a good friend? p26

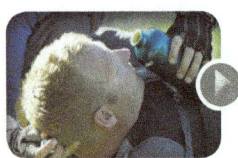
CLIL Mountain rescue p116

Vocabulary
- Priorities
- Verb + noun collocations
- Performing
- Prepositions of place

Language focus
- should/must
- (don't) have to vs. mustn't

Unit aims

I can ...
- talk about daily routines and priorities.
- understand an article about the importance of sleep.
- understand a radio interview.
- understand an article about special schools.
- offer and accept help.
- write about life at a summer camp.

BE CURIOUS

What can you see in the photo?
Start thinking
- Do you write notes like this to remind you?
- What makes you stressed? What makes you happy?
- How does this picture make you feel?

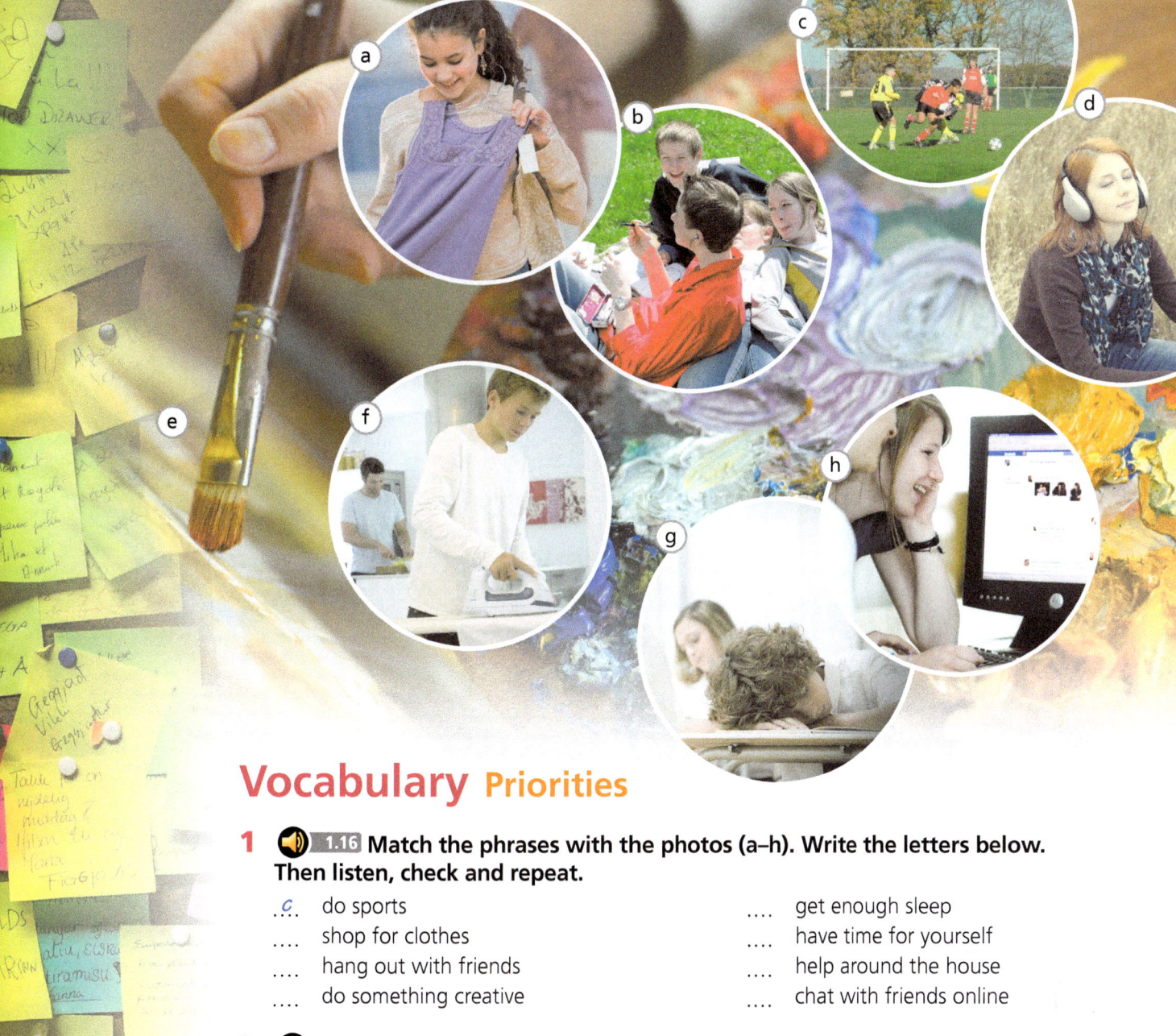

Vocabulary Priorities

1. 🔊 **1.16** Match the phrases with the photos (a–h). Write the letters below. Then listen, check and repeat.

   _c_ do sports
   .... shop for clothes
   .... hang out with friends
   .... do something creative
   .... get enough sleep
   .... have time for yourself
   .... help around the house
   .... chat with friends online

2. 🔊 **1.17** Listen to the teenagers. Match the speakers with the activities in Exercise 1.

   1 *have time for yourself*

3. Think of an adjective or phrase to describe the activities in Exercise 1. Explain your words and phrases to your partner.

   A: I thought of 'boring' for picture a, because I hate shopping for clothes!
   B: For picture a, I thought of 'a day out with my friends' because I love going shopping with them.

Your turn

4. Make notes about the activities in Exercise 1. Then talk to your partner.
   1. Which two things in the list in Exercise 1 are most important to you? Why?
   2. Which things do you argue about with your parents?
   3. Which one thing stresses you most? Why?
   4. Which activities do you have a good time doing?
   5. For which activities do you have to be responsible?

   I think the most important thing for me is having time for myself – so I can just relax and do what I want to do!

➡ **Vocabulary Bank** • page 108

Life is busy with school, homework, sports and other activities and you really need to catch up on your sleep.

Here are three reasons why you should get more sleep:

YOUR BODY NEEDS SLEEP
As a teenager, you *must* get enough sleep – more sleep than an adult. Your body is still growing and your brain is still developing. Experts say that you should get between eight and nine hours of sleep each night.

SLEEP HELPS YOU DO BETTER AT SCHOOL
When you're tired you can't concentrate in your lessons. It's more difficult to learn.

SLEEP KEEPS YOU HEALTHY
Without enough sleep, your body gets weak, and it's easy for you to catch a cold and other illnesses. When you're tired you often eat food with more sugar in it and that isn't good for you.

A GOOD NIGHT'S SLEEP

TEENAGERS WHO GET ENOUGH SLEEP …
- usually have better skin.
- eat less junk food.
- are less likely to experience depression.

Reading A magazine article

1 Work with a partner. Look at the photo and answer the questions.
1 How many hours of sleep do you think teenagers need?
2 What can happen if you don't get enough sleep?

2  **Read the article and check your answers. What's the main aim of the article?**
a To offer advice to teenagers.
b To tell teenagers why their parents complain.

3 Read the article again. Answer the questions.
1 Why do teenagers need more sleep than adults?
2 How many hours of sleep do teenagers need every night?
3 What happens at school if you don't get enough sleep?
4 Why do teens eat unhealthy food when they are tired?
5 What two things should you avoid to get a good night's sleep?

Explore verb + noun collocations

4 Find the collocations in the article. Match verbs (1–6) with nouns (a–f) to form collocations.

1 get   a in your lessons
2 concentrate   b the Internet
3 catch   c more sleep
4 watch   d a snack
5 surf   e a cold
6 have   f TV

➡ **Vocabulary Bank • page 108**

Your turn

5 Ask and answer with your partner.
1 What time do you usually go to bed during the week?
2 Do you find it difficult to get to sleep? Why/Why not?
3 Do you like sleeping late at the weekend?
4 Do you think you get enough sleep? What things stop you sleeping?

I usually go to bed at …
I find it difficult to get to sleep, because …
I love sleeping late at the weekend! I usually get up at …
I don't always get enough sleep, because …

How to get a good night's sleep:

- You shouldn't watch TV, surf the Internet or play computer games before you go to bed. To get to sleep, you need to feel relaxed.

- If you're hungry, have a light snack. You mustn't eat a big meal before you go to bed – it will keep you awake.

- You shouldn't drink any drinks with caffeine or sugar in the evening.

FACT! Some high schools in the US start classes later so that students can sleep a little longer.

Language focus 1
should/must

1 Complete the examples from the text on page 20. Then complete the rules in the box.

1 You .... get enough sleep.
2 You .... get between eight and nine hours of sleep each night.
3 You .... watch TV before you go to bed.

We use ¹.... to say what we think is a good idea and ².... to say what we think is necessary.

➔ Grammar reference • page 100

2 Complete the sentences below with *should* or *shouldn't* and the verbs in the box.

say ~~get~~ go to bed spend

1 How many hours of sleep *should* people *get* every week?
2 Teenagers .... at least an hour a day doing something relaxing.
3 You .... late the night before an important exam.
4 What .... you .... to your parents to convince them that you need more sleep?

3 Complete the sentences with *must* or *mustn't*.

1 You *must* see the sleep project they uploaded on the school website. It's great!
2 I .... forget to take my project to school tomorrow. I forgot it yesterday and today!
3 What .... parents do to make sure their children are getting enough sleep?
4 You .... come to my party this weekend. I really want you there!

4 🔊 1.19 Complete the conversation with the correct words. Then listen and check.

A: Are you coming out on Friday?
B: No. My parents have told me I ¹(should)/ shouldn't (it's a good idea) stay in this weekend. I really ² must / mustn't study for that Maths exam. I can't fail another one.
A: Life isn't all about Maths. You ³ must / should hang out with your friends too.
B: Yes, but I'm really tired.
A: Well, you ⁴ should / shouldn't go to bed so late!
B: Yes, but what about the Maths exam?
A: Your parents are right. You ⁵ mustn't / shouldn't fail the next Maths exam and you ⁶ must / should relax before you go to bed.
B: Okay! I really ⁷ must / mustn't get back to my books. I ⁸ should / shouldn't even be talking to you! Good night!

Your turn

5 Think of two problems. Make notes.

I want to get a dog but my parents don't like the idea. What should I do?

I argued with my best friend and now s/he won't speak to me. What should I do?

6 Work with a partner. Talk about your problems and give advice for each situation.

If your parents don't like dogs, you mustn't get one! You should try to speak to her in a few days' time.

Learn about a new invention.
- What kind of machine are the inventors trying to build?
- What will the machine do?
- What do you think of the machine they build?

2.1 Get up and go!

Listening A radio interview

1 Work with a partner. Look at the photos and answer the questions.
  1 What sort of singer do you think she is learning to be?
  2 What do you think she has to learn?

2 🔊 1.20 Listen to an interview with Jenny Gregson. Check your answers to the questions in Exercise 1.

3 🔊 1.20 Listen again. Complete the notes.

My week	
Every day	1 ..*piano*.. practice 2 .... exercises 3 ....
Tuesday/Thursday	4 .... lessons 5 study ....
Monday/Wednesday/Friday	6 .... lessons
Saturday	7 .... classes 8 .... classes

Vocabulary Performing

4 🔊 1.21 Complete the sentences with the words in the box. Then listen, check and repeat.

> orchestra   act   instruments   ~~voice~~
> plays the piano   dancing   on stage   microphone

  1 Have you heard Paul singing? He's got a really powerful ..*voice*.. .
  2 When the band played the last song, everybody was .... .
  3 Jenny .... very well. She practises a lot.
  4 We went to the Concert Hall last night. The .... played beautifully.
  5 Nobody could hear her singing because the .... was broken.
  6 When the singer came ...., she looked very nervous.
  7 You play the piano and the guitar. Do you play any other .... ?
  8 Keanu Reeves is very handsome but can he .... ?

➡ **Say it right!** • page 96

Your turn

5 Ask and answer with your partner.
  1 Can you sing, dance, act or play an instrument?
  2 Have you ever done any of these activities on stage or in public? How did you feel?
  3 Are you learning to do something new?

> I can play the piano.

> I played the piano at a school concert once. I was very nervous.

> I'm learning to play the guitar. I'm not very good at it!

➡ **Vocabulary Bank** • page 108

Language focus 2 *(don't) have to*

1 **Complete the examples from the listening on page 22. Then choose the words to complete the rule.**

	Present	Past
+	I .... practise every day. She **has to do** voice exercises.	I **had to** sing with a microphone. She **had to** train for many years.
–	We .... dance.	I **didn't have to** learn a new song.
?	.... you .... take singing lessons? **Does** she **have to** go to piano lessons?	**Did** you **have to** sing that song? **Did** she **have to** learn Italian?

> We use *have to* to **say what is necessary to do / give someone a choice of what to do.**

➡ **Grammar reference** • page 100

2 🔊 **1.25** **Complete the sentences with the correct form of *(don't) have to* and the verbs in the box. Then listen and check.**

> practise   make   go (x2)   not take   not go

Dad: Amy, can you come and help me in the kitchen, please?
Amy: Sorry Dad, I ¹ *have to go* somewhere.
Dad: ² .... you .... right now? Can't it wait?
Amy: I promised to go round to Joe's house. He ³ .... for his music exam. He needs me to help him.
Dad: It's just that I ⁴ .... a cake for your grandfather's birthday and I need some help.
Amy: OK then, but please tell Mum I ⁵ .... the dog for a walk this afternoon.
Dad: OK, thanks! The dog ⁶ .... out until this evening. I can take him.
Amy: OK, great!

Your turn

3 **Work with a partner. Ask questions using *Do you have to … ?***
- tidy your room
- get up early at weekends
- practise a musical instrument
- look after your younger brother or sister
- study at the weekend
- wash your parents' car
- train for a sport
- prepare for a show or concert

A: *Do you have to tidy your room?*
B: *Yes, I have to tidy it every week.*

don't have to vs. *mustn't*

4 **Look at the example sentences and complete the rules.**
- We **don't have to** dance.
- You **mustn't talk** too much.

> We use ¹ .... to say it's not necessary to do something.
> We use ² .... to say it's important **not** to do something.

➡ **Grammar reference** • page 100

5 🔊 **1.26** **Complete the letter with *don't have to* or *mustn't* and the verbs in the box. Then listen and check.**

> dance   bring   speak   wear   forget

Dear Students

The school disco is this Friday at 7 pm. Please remember that you ¹ .... to ask your parents for permission. They ² .... to your teacher (it's not necessary – just sign the form). You ³ .... school uniform but you must wear suitable clothing. Also, you ⁴ .... friends from other schools – they aren't allowed in the school. Finally, don't forget – you ⁵ ...., but it's much more fun if you do!!

Discover Culture

Find out about life on the stage.

Discovery EDUCATION

2.2 A life on Broadway

1 **Work with a partner. Look at the photos and answer the questions.**
   1 In which famous street in New York do they perform musicals and plays?
   2 How do you think child actors lives are different to yours? Think about school, social activities, money.

2 ▶ 2.2 **Watch the video and check your answers to question 1.**

3 ▶ 2.2 **Watch the video again. What subjects do they talk about?**
   - Being a popular celebrity
   - Working long hours
   - Living away from home
   - Studying for exams
   - Earning a lot of money
   - Performing for judges

4 ▶ 2.2 **Watch the video again and choose the correct words.**
   1 Many kids dream of **being a director / performing** on Broadway.
   2 Many children train **full-time / part-time** to be actors and performers.
   3 A lot of them leave home **before / when** they are teenagers.
   4 **Most / Some** child actors earn a lot of money.
   5 The set designer **decides / explains** what goes on stage.
   6 The lighting designer helps **invent / create** the world of the play.
   7 The best moment for actors is when the audience **claps / laughs**.

5 **Test your memory. Are the sentences true or false? Correct the false ones.**
   1 Annie has blond hair and blue eyes.
   2 Her dog is big and light brown.
   3 The girls are cleaning the floor with a brush and a bucket of water.
   4 The special effects include rain and snow.

6 ▶ 2.2 **Watch the video again and check your answers.**

Your turn

7 **Discuss the questions with your partner.**
   1 Which do you think are advantages and disadvantages of being a child actor?
   2 Are there any theatre schools near where you live?
   3 Would you like to attend a theatre school? Why/Why not?

Reading   An article

1. Work with a partner. Look at the photos. Why do you think boys and girls want to go to these schools?

2. 🔊 1.27 Read about the football academy La Masia and the Royal Ballet School. Find three ways in which the schools are similar.

3. Read the article again. Which school do the sentences describe? Write LM (La Masia), RB (Royal Ballet) or B (both).
   1. The school only has boys.   LM
   2. Students have normal school and training.
   3. They have time off in the evenings.
   4. The school also has international students.
   5. They have a rest in the afternoon.
   6. To get into the school, they have to show how good they are.

Explore   prepositions

4. Look at the highlighted words in the text. Complete the sentences with the words in the box.

   | of | in front of | between | near | until | over |

   1. At our school concerts, we sing .... our parents and friends.
   2. There are .... 10 international students in my class.
   3. My class is full .... really talented dancers.
   4. We have lessons .... two o'clock and then we practise dancing.
   5. The school isn't .... to where many children live, so they live with other families.
   6. The school is for boys and girls .... the ages of 11 and 16.

   ➡ **Vocabulary Bank** • page 108

Your turn

5. Ask and answer with your partner.
   1. Are there any schools like these in your country?
   2. Would you like to go to a school like these ones? Why?/Why not?
   3. Would you like to live away from home?
   4. What would you miss most?

   I think there are football academies in my country.

6. Write about a time when you won or when you were successful at something. How did you feel?

   I remember once …
   I felt great because …

La Masia Football Academy, BARCELONA

La Masia is Barcelona's football academy. Some of the greatest footballers in the world have come from La Masia. The World Cup and the European Championships were full **of** players from this academy. There are about 80 boys **between** the ages of 11 and 18 at the academy. They go to school **until** half past two in the afternoon, then they have lunch and a siesta. Most boys have to use this time to study and do their homework. In the evening, they watch TV or play video games before they go to bed. For these boys, football is their life. They train hard because they want to be the best.

FACT! *The amount of energy needed to perform a ballet is about the same as playing two full football matches or running almost 29 kilometres.*

The Royal Ballet School, LONDON

The Royal Ballet School in the heart of London trains dancers and choreographers. The school has two buildings, one **near** Richmond Park for 11 to 16-year-olds and the other in Covent Garden for older students. Students at the school mix normal school subjects with their dance classes. Many famous ballet dancers have come from this school. To get into the school, students have to audition – they have to perform **in front of** judges from the school. **Over** 2,000 children attended auditions for the school in 2012. About 70 boys and girls get a place each year. There are students from all over the world. In the evening, when students aren't in class or practising ballet, they can play tennis or play table football in the student halls.

Speaking Offering to help

Real talk: What makes a good friend?

1 ▶ 2.3 Watch the teenagers in the video. What activities do you hear? What do you think makes a good friend?
- helps with decisions
- likes to talk on the phone
- thinks of other people and is helpful
- buys good birthday presents
- has to just be there
- is honest
- likes to go out on the weekend
- helps with homework
- listens
- does all the same activities

2 What do *you* think makes a good friend?

3 🔊 1.28 Laura is talking to Olivia, a new student at her school. What does Laura offer to do?

4 Complete the conversation with the useful language.

Useful language

Offering to help
Here, let me show you.
What do you need?
I'll give you a hand.
All you have to do is …

Asking for help
I'm not sure how to …
Can I ask you something?

5 🔊 1.28 Listen again and check your answers.

6 Work with a partner. Practise the conversation in Exercise 4.

7 Work with a partner. Prepare a conversation like the one in Exercise 4. Use the useful language and your own ideas. Practise the conversation with your partner.

Olivia: Hey, Laura. Can I ¹ *ask you* something?
Laura: Yeah, sure. What's up?
Olivia: It's this Science project. I'm ² …. …. to organise it.
Laura: Mr Brown's put instructions on the school Intranet. What do ³ …. …. ?
Olivia: Well, how do I get access to the Intranet?
Laura: You have to type in your password. Here, let ⁴ …. …. you.
Olivia: Thanks. That's really nice of you!
Laura: It's simple. All you have ⁵ …. …. is follow the instructions and format it correctly.
Olivia: Oh no! I'm not very good at things like that.
Laura: Don't worry. I'll ⁶ …. a hand if you like.
Olivia: Great! Thanks a lot.

Situation 1
You want to download a video but you don't know how.

Student A Explain the problem.

Student B Help Student A. Give him/her ideas about how to find the video, save or download it and where to save it.

Situation 2
You can't find any material for a school project.

Student B Explain the problem.

Student A Help Student B Give him/her help on where to find ideas, i.e. the Internet, the library or interviewing people.

✏️ Writing   A competition entry

1 Look at the photos and read Jon's competition entry. What were his favourite things about summer camp?

 **COMPETITION!!**

WIN A FREE WEEK AT OUR SUMMER CAMP!
Did you go to summer camp? Tell us about your stay. We publish the best ones on our website!

I didn't want to go to summer camp. I imagined an awful place with lots of rules, so Beaufort Camp was a big surprise. We didn't have to get up early and there was plenty of time for breakfast before we started activities at 10 o'clock. There were lots to choose from and they were fun. My favourites were canoeing, volleyball and horse riding. At night, we sat round a fire and we could even sleep outside if we wanted to! The weather was boiling but there was a big swimming pool to cool us down. For me, camp was an incredible experience. I made lots of friends. You should try it!

JONZ

2 Look back at Jon's competition entry again. What does Jon write about?
- favourite activities (daytime / at night)
- the monitors / other campers
- the daily routine
- why he liked it
- the food
- the weather

Useful language

Avoiding repetition (1)
We can use reference words so that we don't repeat the same word.
*We started activities at 10 o'clock. There were **lots** (of activities) to choose from, and **they** (these activities) were fun.*

3 Look at the Useful language box. Find one other way of avoiding repetition of the word *activities* in the text in Exercise 1.

4 Change the phrases in bold in the text so you don't repeat the words.
The best thing about wild camping was the *animals*. There were lots of ¹ **animals** if you looked carefully. On the second day, I saw some *falcons*. ² **The falcons** flew over the trees near the campsite. But the most active animals were *the goats*. ³ **The goats** jump up and down the mountains incredibly fast! I was also amazed at ⁴ **the goats'** huge horns.

✏️ Get writing

PLAN

5 Plan your competition entry for the camp website. Include information from Exercise 2 to help you. Decide what order you are going to put them in.

WRITE

6 Write your competition entry for the camp website. Use your notes from Exercise 5 and the model text to help you.

CHECK

7 Can you say YES to these questions?
- Is the information from Exercise 2 in your email?
- Have you avoided a lot of repetition?

1-2 Review

Vocabulary

1 Write the extreme weather words for each picture.

1 *boiling*

2 Complete the sentences with the words in the box. There are two extra words.

> sleeping bag   camera   first aid kit
> penknife   ~~sun cream~~   compass   torch

1 You need *sun cream* to protect your skin against sunburn.
2 You need a …. to find your way in the dark.
3 You need a warm …. if you're camping.
4 You need a …. to find the correct direction.
5 You need a …. in case you get hurt.

3 Complete the sentences with the correct form of the phrases in the box.

> help around the house   get enough sleep
> hang out with friends   do something creative
> ~~shop for clothes~~   chat with friends online
> do sports   have time for yourself

1 I don't like *shopping for clothes*. I'm not really interested in fashion.
2 I need to be alone sometimes. I like …. myself.
3 I hate …. . Housework is so boring!
4 I …. to stay in touch with them.
5 I dream about …. . I only usually get about 6 hours a night.
6 I want to be a designer or an artist. I'm really happy when I'm …. .
7 I play football for a club and I love swimming. We also …. at school.
8 When I'm not doing homework or with my family I like to …. .

4 Choose the correct words.
1 Lea sings beautifully. She's got a lovely **voice** / microphone.
2 I play the violin in the school **instrument** / **orchestra**.
3 Pete is learning his lines – he's **dancing** / **acting** in the end of term play.
4 Do you play **an instrument** / **the piano**? Yes, I play the **piano** / **instrument**.
5 Our headteacher uses **a microphone** / **an instrument** to talk to us in the hall.
6 Are you nervous before you go **acting** / **on stage**?

 Explore vocabulary

5 Choose the correct words.

> Q: I'm tired during the day – how can I wake up?!
>
> A: ¹ **Catch** / **Get** more sleep. Most people need ² **over** / **above** six hours sleep a night. Don't sit in front of the TV or ³ **surf** / **watch** the Internet before you go to bed.
>
> To help you ⁴ **get more** / **concentrate** in lessons, spend time ⁵ **outdoors** / **indoors** in ⁶ **front of** / **between** lessons and get some fresh air. Also, ⁷ **surf** / **have** a light snack.
>
> Have the windows open in your classroom and sit ⁸ **beside** / **over** the window. When you are ⁹ **indoors** / **outdoors** all day it makes you feel sleepy.

6 Complete the text with the words in the box.

> in   sub-zero conditions   on (x2)   rises
> falls   catch   of

When should I travel to New Zealand?

You may think that New Zealand is one of the warmest places ¹ *on* the planet, but New Zealand is full ² …. surprises! In summer, the temperature ³ …. to an average maximum temperature of between 20 and 30°C, but the temperature ⁴ …. as you travel south. While the far north has subtropical weather during summer, inland alpine areas of South Island can experience ⁵ …. as low as -10°C in winter. So wrap up warm if you don't want to ⁶ …. a cold! One year the people ⁷ …. the island experienced 40cm of snow ⁸ …. total in one night.

28

Language focus

1 Complete the sentences with the present continuous or present simple of the verbs in the box.

| read   do   not stay   rain   get   ~~study~~   stay |

1 We _are studying_ Japanese at school this term.
2 .... they .... a test right now?
3 They .... up late if they have school the next day.
4 It's nearly the end of September and the weather .... colder.
5 What book .... you .... at the moment?
6 I prefer to .... indoors when it's cold
7 It hardly ever .... in the winter.
8 You look tired. .... you .... enough sleep?

2 Complete the sentences and questions with the verbs in brackets. Use the past continuous or past simple.

1 I _saw_ (see) sharks when I _was swimming_ (swim) in the ocean.
2 Jake .... (climb) in the mountains when he .... (drop) his camera.
3 They .... (walk) in the desert when they .... (find) a huge cave.
4 What .... you .... (do) when I .... (phone) you yesterday?
5 It .... (not rain) when we .... (start) hiking.
6 Where .... you .... (jog) when you .... (lose) your mobile?

3 Complete the sentences with the words in the box.

| should try   ~~mustn't tell~~   shouldn't stay up |
| must finish   should/get   mustn't be |

1 You _mustn't tell_ people your password when you surf the Internet.
2 Anna .... to concentrate more in lessons.
3 We .... this school project before Friday.
4 When you chat online you .... unkind to friends.
5 They .... so late doing their homework.
6 How many hours' sleep .... people .... in your opinion?

4 Choose the correct word.

1 You (**don't have to**) / **mustn't** practise every day.
2 They **don't have to** / **mustn't** chat to strangers on the Internet.
3 We **don't have to** / **mustn't** sing that song – we can choose a different one.
4 **Do you have to** / **Must you** tidy your room at the weekends?

UNIT 1–2

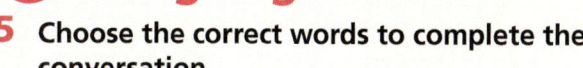 Language builder

5 Choose the correct words to complete the conversation.

Sylvia:	Hi, Kylie! ¹ _b_ your homework?
Kylie:	No, I ² .... at my photos from my holiday.
Sylvia:	I ³ .... that too. ⁴ .... have fun on your holiday?
Kylie:	Yes! We ⁵ .... to the mountains. One day, while we ⁶ ...., some wild deer ⁷ .... up to us to find food.
Sylvia:	Amazing! I want to go hiking next summer holiday. What ⁸ .... take with me?
Kylie:	Well you ⁹ .... take anything too heavy. You ¹⁰ .... take a map because that's on your smartphone. But you ¹¹ .... watch out for snakes.
Sylvia:	Snakes? I don't like snakes!

1	a Do you do	b Are you doing	c Do you doing
2	a am look	b looking	c am looking
3	a usually do	b do usually	c am usually doing
4	a You did	b Did you	c Were you
5	a went	b go	c were going
6	a hiked	b were hiking	c hike
7	a come	b were coming	c came
8	a I should	b should I	c do I should
9	a should	b must	c shouldn't
10	a have to	b don't have to	c should
11	a must	b shouldn't	c don't have to

Speaking

6 Match the sentences.

1 I'll give you a hand. _e_
2 I think this city is a great place to live!
3 Can I ask you something?
4 Maybe living in a village isn't all bad.
5 I'm not sure how to use this computer.
6 I reckon that this town is really boring.

a Let me show you.
b OK, perhaps you're right.
c I agree. There are lots of things to do here.
d I disagree. There are lots of things to do here.
e That's really kind.
f Yeah, sure. What's up?

29

3 Art all around us

In this unit ...

The art of storytelling **p33**

A world of music **p36**

Have you ever been to a concert? **p38**

CLIL Perspective **p117**

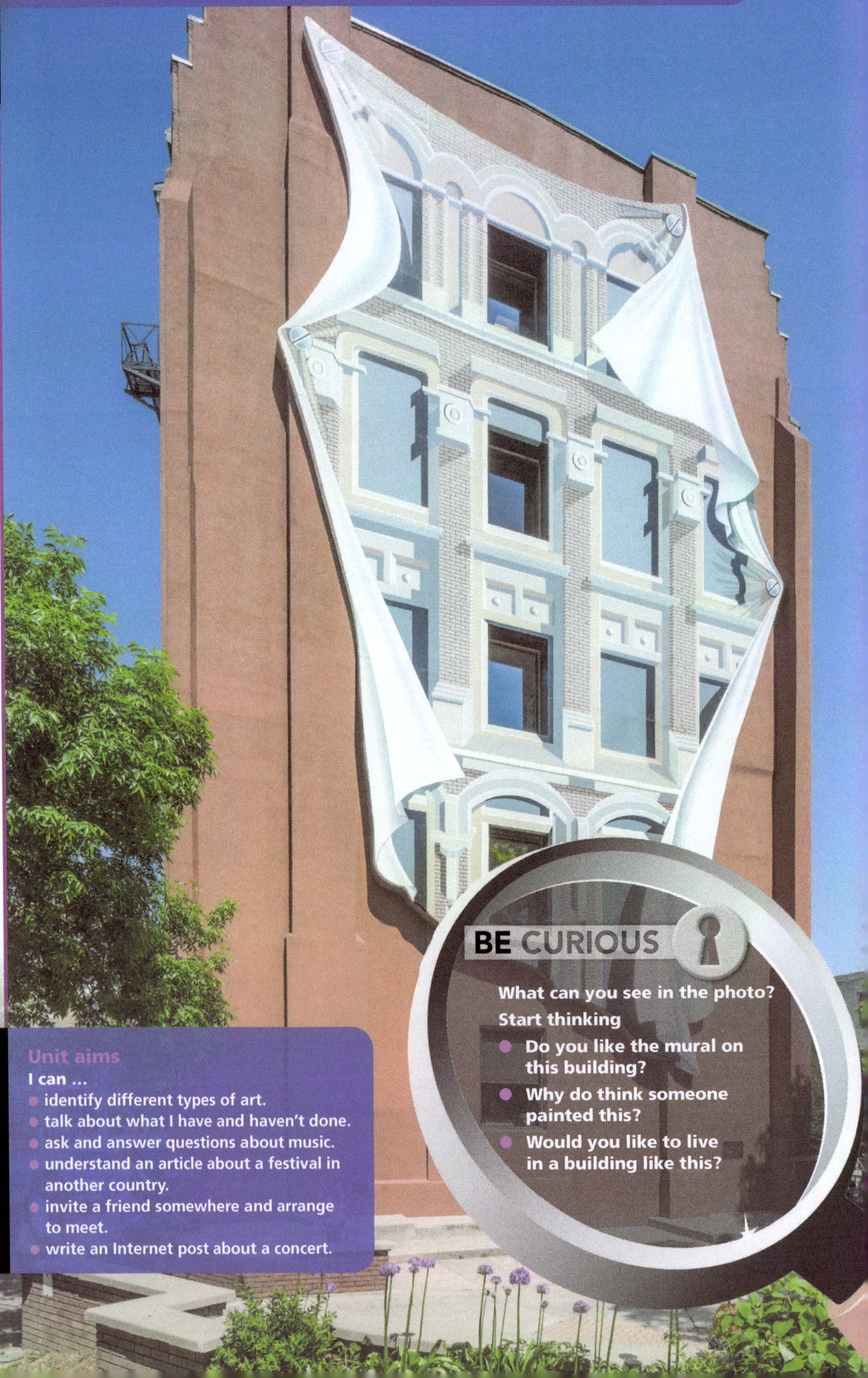

Vocabulary
- Art around us
- Collocations
- Musical instruments
- Phrasal verbs with *up*

Language focus
- Present perfect for indefinite past time
- Present perfect with *ever/never*

Unit aims
I can ...
- identify different types of art.
- talk about what I have and haven't done.
- ask and answer questions about music.
- understand an article about a festival in another country.
- invite a friend somewhere and arrange to meet.
- write an Internet post about a concert.

BE CURIOUS

What can you see in the photo?
Start thinking
- Do you like the mural on this building?
- Why do think someone painted this?
- Would you like to live in a building like this?

Vocabulary Art around us

1 🔊 1.29 Match the words in the box with the art around us (a–j). Which word describes where we see paintings? Then listen, check and repeat.

> concert hall   busker   living statue   juggler   sculpture   mural
> exhibition   gallery   painting   graffiti   portrait painter

a *busker*

2 Complete the chart with the words from Exercise 1.

works of art	places to see art or music	a performer or an artist
		busker

3 🔊 1.30 Listen to two groups on a day trip in London. What did each group see? Write the words from Exercise 1 in your notebook.
Group 1: *gallery*
Group 2:

Your turn

4 Ask and answer with your partner.
  1 Which of the people, places and things in Exercise 1 can you find near where you live?
  2 Do you like watching street performers like jugglers and human statues? Why?/Why not?
There's a gallery of modern art quite near my house, but I don't go there very often!

👁 **Get it right!**

When we use *there* after *go*, we don't use the preposition *to*.
We go **there** three times a week.
Did you go **there** on your own?

➡ Vocabulary Bank • page 109

Reading An online debate

1 Work with a partner. Look at the pictures below. What do you think makes a person an artist?

2 🔊 1.31 Read the debate. What do Josh and Kirsten think art is?

3 Read the article again. Are these sentences true or false? Correct the false sentences.
   1 Josh likes doing graffiti. *F*
   2 To Josh, photographs that people post online aren't examples of art.
   3 Josh and his friends like the portraits he draws and the photos he takes.
   4 Kirsten enjoys going to art museums.
   5 Kirsten believes that art is anything that is creative and fun.
   6 Kirsten thinks that good art is easy.

Explore collocations

4 Find the collocations in the text. Match the words in box A with the words in box B. Then complete the sentences.

A | post | ~~good~~ | passionate | take | work | make |

B | ~~at~~ | hard | online | photos | about | money |

   1 I love painting, but I'm not very ..*good at*.. it – some of my pictures are terrible!
   2 You have to …. to be a good artist.
   3 Is it okay to …. these photos of you …. ?
   4 My sister loves to …. of unusual buildings.
   5 It's very difficult to …. from painting pictures.
   6 My sister's really …. juggling. She practises for hours every day.

➡ **Vocabulary Bank** • page 109

Your turn

5 Work in small groups. Have a debate. Is everyone an artist?
   • Make notes of different examples to support your opinion.
   • Discuss your ideas using your notes.
   • Which group made the best argument?

   I agree, I think graffiti is …
   I'm not sure, I think it depends on …
   There are some great examples of graffiti on …

ARTICLES   CONTACT

EVERYONE'S AN *artist*

YOU'VE TAKEN A PHOTO AND PUT IT ON A SOCIAL NETWORK SITE. FIFTEEN FRIENDS HAVE GIVEN YOU A 'LIKE'. YOU'RE AN ARTIST!

THE CASE FOR:

We look at the *Mona Lisa* or a Picasso painting and we say, 'That's art.' But what about the amazing graffiti someone has painted on your street? What about the poster presentation you've done? You've worked hard and it's great. So, have you made a work of art? To me, art is anything that's creative. Of course, I like going to famous museums but I also like drawing portraits of my friends or taking photos. I'm not very good at these things, but I'm creative. I'm passionate about them, and my friends like them. Most of all, I like them!
Josh, age 15, San Diego, California

THE CASE AGAINST:

I have always loved visiting art museums. Why? Because I like looking at good art. Art is not a drawing that a four-year-old child has done, it isn't painting your body crazy colours and standing in the street, and it certainly isn't graffiti. Some people say, 'If it's creative, it's art.' I don't agree. My aunt is an artist. She went to art school, and she has worked in her studio for years. She hasn't made much money, but her sculptures have been in a few exhibitions. Her art is great. You haven't made a work of art if you haven't studied for years and developed your talent.
Kirsten, age 16, Berlin, Germany

WHAT IS *art*? WHAT'S YOUR OPINION?

FACT! *The British graffiti artist Banksy sold a piece of graffiti for $1.8 million.*

Language focus 1 Present perfect for indefinite past time

1 Complete the examples from the text on page 32. Then choose the words to complete the rule.

1. You <u>'ve taken</u> a photo.
2. What about the poster presentation you …. ?
3. …. you …. a work of art?
4. I …. always …. visiting art museums.
5. She …. much money.
6. You …. …. a work of art if you haven't studied.

We use the present perfect to talk about events in the past when the time **is / is not** important.

 **Grammar reference • page 101**

> **Get it right!**
>
> **gone and been**
> *gone* = to go and not come back
> *been* = to go and come back.
> He's **gone** out. (He's not here now.)
> He's **been** out. (He's back now.)

2 Complete the sentences with an irregular verb from the box. Use the present perfect.

> take   not visit   ~~see~~   meet   go (x2)   play   speak

1. My sister <u>has seen</u> that exhibition three times. She loves it!
2. My grandparents …. to museums all over the world.
3. We …. about ten photos so far.
4. I …. never …. to anyone in English outside class.
5. I …. never …. a famous artist. Have you?
6. He …. to the gallery. He'll be back later.
7. I …. an interesting gallery – they are all very boring!
8. I …. the guitar in three bands.

3 🔊 **1.32** Complete the text with the verbs in brackets. Use the present perfect. Then listen and check.

The Berlin Wall separated East and West Berlin. On the West side, there was lots of political graffiti. Now, some artists ¹<u>have started</u> (start) to recreate the original art. One artist, Bill Neumann explains, 'Well, the idea is very simple. I ² …. (look) at old photos and I ³ …. (make) copies of the graffiti. Other artists ⁴ …. (do) the same thing. We ⁵ …. (recreate) a section of the original wall. It ⁶ …. (be) a really interesting experience for us. We ⁷ …. (not finish) the work, but we hope to soon.'

Your turn

4 Write questions using the prompts.

- see / a busker
- paint / a portrait
- take / a photo of someone famous
- see / good graffiti
- go / concert hall
- post / a photo online
- go / an exhibition

Have you ever seen a busker?

5 Ask and answer with your partner.

> Have you ever seen a busker?

>> Yes, I have. I've seen a lot of them in town. Some of them are very good.

Learn about Aboriginal art.
- What do Australian Aboriginals use art for?
- Why are some paintings like 'survival maps'?
- What is a common feature of Aboriginal art?

3.1 The art of storytelling

Vocabulary Instruments

1 🔊 **1.33** Match the words in the box with the instruments in the pictures (1–14). Then listen, check and repeat.

> guitar   drums   banjo   flute   violin   saxophone
> keyboards   mouth organ   tambourine   piano
> recorder   trumpet   cello   clarinet

2 Work with a partner. Answer the questions.
1 What instruments do you associate with orchestras and classical music?
2 What instruments do you expect to see in a pop or rock band?
3 What about the other instruments: where would you normally see them?

↻ **Vocabulary Bank** • page 109

Listening An interview

3 Look at the picture of a musician called Leo. What instruments has he got? Where do you think he performs?

4 🔊 **1.34** Listen to a journalist, Marcia, interviewing Leo. Check your ideas from Exercise 3.

5 🔊 **1.34** Listen again and answer the questions.
1 Where is Marcia?
2 Why is Leo so well known in Auckland?
3 Which of Leo's instruments is new?
4 How long has he played today?
5 What types of music does he play?
6 Which instruments has he never played?

Your turn

6 Work in groups. Do a music survey. Report your group's information to the class.
- Do you like listening to music?
- What kind of music do you like?
- Do you play a musical instrument?
- Do you ever give money to buskers?

People listen to different kinds of music but ... .
Some people listen to music on the bus and ... .
Two people always give money to buskers because ... .

Language focus 2 Present perfect with *ever/never*

1 **Complete the examples from the listening on page 34.**
  1 He's ......*never*...... played here at the festival.
  2 Have you .... played at this festival?
  3 I've .... played here before.
  4 Have you .... played in a group?
  5 I've .... played the cello or the violin.

➡ **Grammar reference** • page 101

2 **Look at the questions in Exercise 1. Where does *ever* go in the question?**

3 **Rewrite the questions putting *ever* in the right position.**
  1 Have you met a famous musician?
  2 Have you visited England?
  3 Has your town had a music festival?
  4 Have your parents owned a pet?

➡ **Say it right!** • page 96

4 **Make sentences. For pictures 1–3, write sentences using *never*. For pictures 4–6, write questions using *ever*. Ask and answer with your partner.**

1 I / paint / graffiti on a wall
2 he / play / the drums
3 she / win / a race

4 climb / top of a mountain
5 go / a concert
6 paint / a house

5 🔊 1.37 **Write questions using the verbs in brackets. Then listen and check.**

The MUSIC QUIZ

1 you (be) to a concert or festival?
2 you (download) music from the Internet?
3 you (be) in a band?
4 you (sing) in a choir?
5 you (upload) a piece of music to the Internet?
6 you (meet) a famous musician or singer?
7 you (travel) a long way to see a group or singer?
8 you (listen) to music while doing sport at the same time?
9 you (post) a music video online?
10 you (follow) a band on Twitter?

Your turn

6 **Ask and answer the quiz questions in Exercise 5 with your partner.**

> Have you ever been to a concert or festival?

> No, I've never been to a concert but I've been to a festival.

Discover Culture

Australia

India

Mexico

a

b

c

1 Look at the images of three musical instruments (a–c) and complete the table with information below.

Mexico   India   Australia   ~~sitar~~
didgeridoo   trumpet   string   wind (x2)

	Country	Name of instrument	Type of instrument
Photo A			
Photo B		*sitar*	
Photo C			

Find out about unusual instruments.

Discovery EDUCATION

3.2 A world of music

2 ▶ 3.2 Watch the video and check your answers.

3 Match the information to the three different musical traditions or instruments.

Mariachi   didgeridoo   sitar

1 The music is lively and emotional.
2 The instrument has been around for hundreds of years.
3 A famous group used this instrument and musical style in their own music.
4 This music requires a number of different instruments.
5 This is one of the oldest instruments in the world.
6 More Australians play this instrument now.

4 Test your memory. Mark the sentences true or false. Correct the false ones.

1 We see the Mariachi perform live and when they are practising.
2 There are drums, guitars, violins and trumpets in a Mariachi group.
3 The sitar player closes his eyes when he plays.
4 The Australian Aborigine is sitting with three other people.

5 ▶ 3.2 Watch the video again and check your answers.

6 What is the report's main message? Choose the best option.

1 Every country has different musical traditions.
2 We can now share and listen to different musical styles very easily.
3 Music can be happy or sad, choose the music according to your mood.

Your turn

7 Ask and answer in groups.

1 Would you like to play one of these instruments?
2 Are there any traditional instruments which are special to your country?
3 What do you think are the positive things about playing in a band or orchestra with other people?

Reading A web page

UNIT 3

1 Work with a partner. Look at the pictures of a festival in the U.S.A. What do you think people do there?

2 🔊 1.38 Read the text and check your answers to Exercise 1.

3 Read the Frequently Asked Questions (FAQs) about The Burning Man Festival. Match the questions (A–F) to the answers (1–6).

A What else do people do at the festival?
B Has the festival always taken place there?
C What happens after the festival?
D What is The Burning Man Festival?
E How is it different from other festivals?
F Why is it called The Burning Man Festival?

Explore phrasal verbs with *up*

4 Look at the highlighted words in the text. Complete the sentences with the correct form of the words in the box.

| show set ~~tidy~~ pick light dress |

1 When the festival was over, we ….*tidied*…. up all our rubbish and went home.
2 For the festival last year, my friend …. up as a robot.
3 Hundreds of fireworks …. up the sky to end the festival.
4 We asked him to come at eight o'clock but he didn't …. up until nine o'clock.
5 The band …. up their equipment on the stage before the concert.
6 We …. up some food in the supermarket and drove out to the festival site.

➡ **Vocabulary Bank** • page 109

Your turn

5 Ask and answer with your partner.
1 Would you like to go to a festival like The Burning Man? Why?/Why not?
2 Does your school or town have its own festival? What type of festival is it? What can you do there?

> I'd really like to go because it looks amazing in the photos.

6 Write about the last festival you went to.
The last festival I went to was in our town. There were …

Burning Man Festival FAQs

Maybe you've **picked up** tickets to the Festival, but you're not sure what to expect. Read these FAQs to find out more:

1 *D*
It's an arts community festival which takes place every year for a week at the end of August in The Black Rock Desert in Nevada, in the U.S.A. More than 60,000 people **showed up** last year. Volunteers create a community in the desert called Black Rock City – they **set up** everything themselves.

2 ….
No, it started in San Francisco, California in 1986, next to the Golden Gate Bridge. It moved to the desert five years later.

3 ….
Because fire is an important theme of the festival. People build an enormous wooden statue of a person which is more than 30 metres tall and they burn it on the Saturday night of the festival. They also build and burn lots of other things.

4 ….
They **dress up** in costumes and because of the dust in the desert they wear goggles. There are also a lot of other fun activities. There is usually a balloon chain of 450 different balloons which is one kilometre long and it **lights up** the sky.

5 ….
After the festival, the rules are very strict: people must **tidy up** everything and leave the desert exactly as it was before the festival started because the organisers are very worried about protecting the environment.

6 ….
It's unusual because there aren't any famous bands or celebrities. It's all about community – everyone is on the same level.

> **FACT!** Every August, Black Rock City becomes the third largest city in Nevada – but then it disappears in September!

Speaking Invitations and arrangements

Real talk: Have you ever been to a concert?

1. ▶ **3.3** Watch the teenagers in the video. How many of the teenagers …
   a) have been to more than one concert?
   b) prefer to do something else?
   c) have played in a concert?

2. 💬 Have *you* ever been to a concert?

3. 🔊 **1.39** Fran and Nicky are talking. What are they arranging to do?

4. Complete the conversation with the useful language.

Useful language

What time shall we meet (then)?
Yeah, why not?
Do you fancy -ing … ?
Sounds good!

That's a great idea!
Let's go together.
How about -ing … ?
Shall I (ask my dad to get us)?

5. 🔊 **1.39** Listen again and check your answers.

6. 💬 Work with a partner. Practise the conversation in Exercise 4.

7. 💬 Change the words in bold in the conversation. Use the ideas below. Take turns to ask and answer the questions.

Concert 1
The Black Roots
The Hacienda Club
Station Road

Doors open: 9pm   **Band starts:** 9.30

Concert 2
Live concert with Don't be Shy
The Black Bee Club, Miller Street

Doors open: 7.30pm   **Band:** 8pm

Fran:	Nicky, do you ¹ *fancy going* to a concert tomorrow?
Nicky:	Yeah, ²…. ? Who's playing?
Fran:	A **pop rock** band called **The Sweets**. They're a new band. I've got free tickets.
Nicky:	³…. good! Where are they playing?
Fran:	The **Apollo Club**, in **Market Street**.
Nicky:	OK. What time ⁴…. meet then?
Fran:	It starts at **8.30**, I think. ⁵…. together. ⁶…. coming to my house at **half seven**?
Nick:	OK. ⁷…. ask **my dad** to come and get us at the end?
Frank:	Yes, that's a ⁸…. !
Nick:	OK. See you tomorrow, then.

Writing — An internet post

1 Look at the photos and read Alba's blog about a concert. Did she enjoy it?

I've just come back from a fantastic free concert. It was in a park near the city centre and there was a great atmosphere, with hundreds of young people dancing and enjoying themselves. There were lots of bands but for me the best one was The Hurricane from Manchester. They play a mixture of styles. Their first songs were folk and blues but the last ones sounded more like reggae and rock. The singer (Janie Smith) has a really amazing voice, and the guitarists and drummer played together really well. They've just made an album (they've never had a hit) and I want to get it!!! If you get the chance to see them, go for it ☺!

2 Read Alba's description of the concert. Answer the questions.

Does Alba …
1 say where the concert took place?
2 describe the atmosphere?
3 describe the stage?
4 say who played and give information about the band?
5 say what she had to eat or drink at the concert?
6 give her opinion?
7 make a recommendation?
8 say how much it cost?

Useful language

Avoiding repetition (2)
We use *one* (singular) and *ones* (plural) to refer to something we mentioned earlier in a text.
- *There were lots of bands but for me the best **one** was The Hurricane from Manchester.*
- *Their first songs were folk and blues but the last **ones** sounded more like reggae and rock.*

3 Look at the Useful language box. What kind of words do *one* and *ones* replace?

4 Complete the sentences with *one* or *ones*.
1 I really liked the last band. The first ....*ones*.... weren't as good.
2 There are two boys in the band. The tall .... plays the drums.
3 They sang two songs. Which .... did you like best?
4 I've seen them in concert twice. The last .... was in the park last summer.
5 I like all their songs but the earlier .... are great to dance to.
6 Dave's got three guitars: a red .... and two black .... .

Get writing

PLAN

5 Plan a blog post about a concert you've been to. Use Exercise 2 to help you. Decide what order to put them in.

WRITE

6 Write your blog post about the concert. Use your notes from Exercise 5 and the model text to help you.

CHECK

7 Can you say YES to these questions?
- Is the information from the list in Exercise 2 in your writing?
- Have you avoided using repetition?

4 Adventure

Discovery EDUCATION

In this unit ...

- The age of discovery p43
- The strange and beautiful land of Australia p46 
- Exciting activities p48 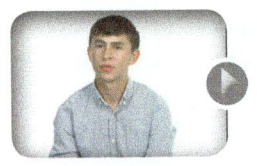
- CLIL Where in the world? p118 

Vocabulary
- Expressions with *go*
- Words from the text
- Phrasal verbs
- Interesting adjectives

Language focus
- Present perfect with *still*, *yet*, *already* and *just*
- Present perfect with *for* and *since*
- Present perfect and past simple

Unit aims
I can ...
- talk about activities.
- understand an online information advertisement about a charity adventure holiday.
- understand a radio interview with teenagers on a school trip.
- understand about culture and customs in New Zealand.
- ask for and understand information about an adventure activity.
- write a travel blog.

BE CURIOUS

What can you see in the photo?
Start thinking
- What are the men doing?
- What kind of holiday is it?
- What activities do you think they will do?

40

Vocabulary Expressions with *go*

1 🔊 **1.40** Match the phrases in the box with the photos (a–i). Then listen, check and repeat.

> climbing   a theme park   summer camp   ~~a school exchange~~
> a guided tour   a safari   skiing   sailing   trekking

a *a school exchange*

2 🔊 **1.41** Listen to the conversation between Chloe and Ben. Where did they go last summer?

3 🔊 **1.41** Listen again and complete the chart with the words in Exercise 1.

go	go on	go to
		a summer camp

4 Look again at the expressions in Exercise 1 and think about the trips. On which trips do you usually a) do an activity? b) sleep away from home? c) use some kind of transport?

You do an activity when you go climbing.
You sleep away from home when you go to a summer camp.

Your turn

5 You and your partner went on a summer camp last year. Choose four activities that you did at the camp from Exercise 1. Ask and answer questions to find out which activities your partner did.

> Did you go climbing?

> Yes, I did. / No I didn't.

➡ **Vocabulary Bank** • page 110

Reading An online advertisement

1 Look at the photos. What are the teenagers doing on the boat? What kind of trip is it?

2 🔊 1.42 Read the online advertisement and check your answers.

3 Read the advertisement again. What does each of the numbers in the box refer to?

> two or three hundred   thousands   30   70 (x2)   40   15   200

Explore words in context

4 Match these words and phrases from the advertisement with the definitions below.

> an exact copy   a taste of   disabled   take it in turns
> keep watch   adjusted   cool stuff

1 stay awake and look out for danger
2 a short experience of something different
3 a very good imitation
4 exciting things to do
5 share the work with other people
6 a condition that makes it difficult to do things most people can do
7 change the way you behave or think

Your turn

5 Ask and answer with your partner. Describe a time when you did something for the first time.
- Where were you?
- What did you do for the first time?
- How did you feel?

> I remember the first time I went skiing … It was really cool!

6 Write a paragraph beginning *I remember the first time I … .*

> *I remember the first time I went sailing. It was a beautiful day but I was very nervous because I didn't know how to swim! …*

LIFE ON THE WAVES

'I've never sailed before. This is my first time and it's an amazing feeling.' Sandra, 16, is on The Stavros S Niarchos, a 200 ft (70 metre) sailing ship, with 40 other young sailors. The Stavros is an exact copy of the ships that pirates sailed two or three hundred years ago. It belongs to the Tall Ships Youth Trust. The Trust offers sailing trips for teenagers and young adults. Every year, thousands of young people get their first taste of the sea. Up to 70% of them are disabled or disadvantaged. For everyone, it's a once in a lifetime experience!

Sandra is on a trip from the Azores, in the North Atlantic, to Spain. The trip lasts a week and they have already been at sea for three days. 'We do everything,' she explained. 'We take the wheel, we cook, we clean and we take it in turns to keep watch at night. I never knew there was so much work on a ship!'

Her friend, Emma, 15, has never been on a boat before either. 'I still haven't adjusted to life at sea.' 'We've done some cool stuff,' says James, 17. 'I've just climbed up and down the mast. It's 30 metres tall and the views are

Language focus 1 Present perfect
with *still, yet, already* and *just*

UNIT 4

1 Complete the examples from the text on page 42.

+	They .... **already** .... at sea for three days. I .... **just** .... up and down the mast.
–	I **still** .... to life at sea. We .... any whales **yet**.
?	**Have** you **seen** any dolphins **yet**? How long **have** you **been** at sea?

➔ Grammar reference • page 102

2 Look at the chart and complete the sentences using *still, yet, already* and *just*.

1. I'm sorry but the ship has .... *already* .... left. It left about an hour ago.
2. I .... haven't seen any dolphins and we've been on this boat all morning.
3. Has the boat left the port .... ?
4. We've .... come back from a week at sea. It was amazing!
5. The passengers .... haven't got on the ship.
6. We haven't done any training .... . We're starting this afternoon.
7. Don't go into the ship's kitchen, please. I've .... cleaned it.
8. She's .... been on three trips this year.

3 Use the cues to make dialogues with *already, just* and *yet*.

1. A: you/check/passport?
   Have you checked your passport yet?
   B: Yes, but (not/pack rucksack).
   Yes, but I haven't ...
2. A: your friend Sam/pick up/tickets?
   B: No, but .... (already/buy/them).
3. A: you/decide/take/phone or tablet?
   B: Yes, ... (just/pack it).
4. A: your friend Sam/book/taxi?
   B: No, but .... (yet/have got the number).
5. A: you/write down/emergency number?
   B: Yes, ... (just/write/the notepaper).

4 🔊 1.43 Complete the text using the words in brackets and the present perfect. Then listen and check.

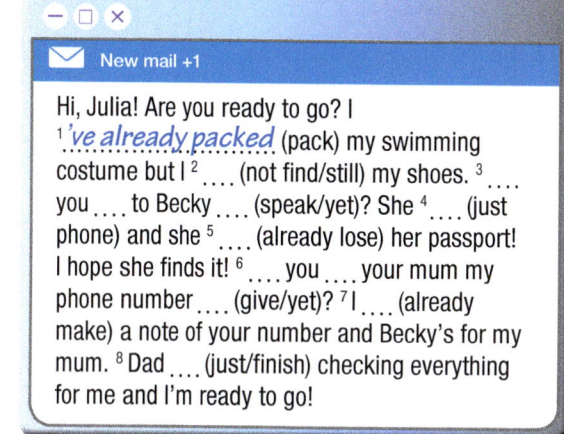

> New mail +1
>
> Hi, Julia! Are you ready to go? I ¹ *'ve already packed* (pack) my swimming costume but I ² .... (not find/still) my shoes. ³ .... you .... to Becky .... (speak/yet)? She ⁴ .... (just phone) and she ⁵ .... (already lose) her passport! I hope she finds it! ⁶ .... you .... your mum my phone number .... (give/yet)? ⁷ I .... (already make) a note of your number and Becky's for my mum. ⁸ Dad .... (just/finish) checking everything for me and I'm ready to go!

Your turn

5 Use the activities in the box to write five questions using *already, still, just* and *yet*.

> brush your teeth   do all your homework
> watch TV   play computer games
> tidy your room   read a book
> send a text message   take a photo

Have you brushed your teeth yet?

6 Ask and answer your questions with your partner. The person who gets the most *Yes* answers wins.

> Have you brushed your teeth yet?
>
> Yes, I have. / No, I haven't.

incredible! We've seen dolphins and turtles. We haven't seen any whales yet, but the captain says there are whales near the Spanish coast. This is definitely the best thing I've ever done!'

If you want to know more about the Tall Ships Youth Trust, visit their website at www.tallships.org

FACT! Over 95,000 people have sailed 1.8 million nautical miles with the Tall Ships Youth Trust.

Learn about Magellan the explorer.
- Why did Magellan go to live with the king and queen of Portugal?
- Why did Europeans want to go to Asia?
- What was Magellan's plan? Did he succeed?

Discovery EDUCATION

4.1 The age of discovery

Listening An interview

1 Work with a partner. Look at the photo of some teenagers on a school trip in Paris. What kind of things do you think they've done on their trip so far?

2 🔊 **1.44** Listen to the conversations. Which sentence best summarises how the teenagers feel about the trip?
- a They all love everything about the trip.
- b They think the trip is really boring.
- c They like some things on the trip more than others.

3 🔊 **1.44** Listen again and answer the questions.
1. When did they arrive?
2. How long have they been in Paris?
3. How did they get to the top of the Eiffel Tower?
4. Have they visited any museums?
5. Have they done any shopping?
6. How's their French?
7. When is their last day?
8. What do they want to do on their last day?

Vocabulary Phrasal verbs

4 🔊 **1.45** Match the phrasal verbs (1–6) with their synonyms (a–f). Then listen, check and repeat.
1. I really want to **come back**.
2. We've **picked up** lots of French.
3. Our bus **set off** at 5 am.
4. They want us to **find out** for ourselves.
5. We're going to **look round** the shops.
6. We've been so busy, we all just want to **chill out**.

a discover
b explore
c relax
d learn in an informal way
e start on a journey
f return

> 👁 **Get it right!**
> We can separate some phrasal verbs. Use a good dictionary to check.
> We've **picked up** a lot of French.
> We've **picked** a lot of French **up**.
> With object pronouns we say:
> We picked **it** up. (not ~~We picked up it~~.)

5 Complete the sentences with the correct form of the verbs in Exercise 4.
1. On the guided tour of the museum, we ..*found out*.. all about tall ships.
2. While my dad was in Argentina, he .... a bit of Spanish.
3. While I .... that bookshop, I found this travel guide for Dublin.
4. This is a terrible restaurant. I don't think I will .... here ever again!
5. You're really nervous. Why don't you ....?
6. We have to .... early if we want to get to Cambridge before lunch.

➔ **Say it right!** • page 96

Your turn

6 Think of a place you visited. Make notes. Try to use the phrasal verbs.

I've visited Rome in Italy. I didn't pick up any Italian.

7 Ask and answer about the place you visited with your partner.

➔ **Vocabulary Bank** • page 110

Language focus 2 Present perfect with *for* or *since*

1 Complete the examples from the listening on page 44. Then complete the rules.

We've been here	1	two days. five minutes. a long time. three years.
	2	Tuesday. three o'clock. March. 2012.

> We use .... with periods of time and .... when we talk about a specific time.

➡ Grammar reference • page 102

2 Look at the table and complete the sentences with *for* or *since*.

1. I've been in Paris .... two days and I haven't seen the Eiffel Tower yet!
2. We set off early but we've only been on the bus .... an hour.
3. I haven't seen our teachers .... 10 o'clock this morning.
4. I'd love to go to Disneyland Paris – I haven't been there .... I was five.
5. I have studied French .... five years and I can understand quite a lot.
6. Helen's picked up a lot of French .... she's been in Paris.
7. We haven't eaten any French food .... we got here!
8. My teacher hasn't been to Paris .... ten years and she's a bit lost!

Present perfect and past simple

3 Complete the examples from the listening on page 44.

A: When ¹ *did* you .... (get) here?
B: On Tuesday, we ² .... (set off) at 5 am! We ³ .... (be) here for two full days. This is our third day
A: ⁴ .... you .... (be) up the tower yet?
B: Yes, we ⁵ .... (go) up about an hour ago.

➡ Grammar reference • page 102

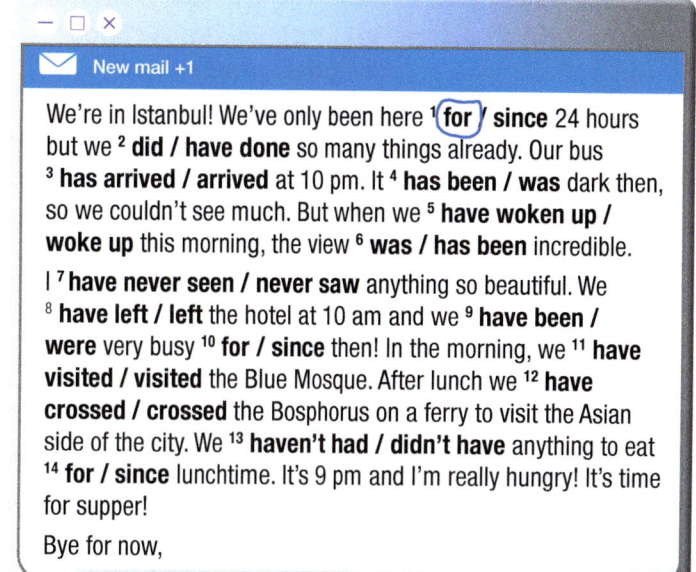

4 🔊 1.48 Choose the correct words to complete the text. Then listen and check.

> **New mail +1**
>
> We're in Istanbul! We've only been here ¹ **for** / since 24 hours but we ² **did / have done** so many things already. Our bus ³ **has arrived / arrived** at 10 pm. It ⁴ **has been / was** dark then, so we couldn't see much. But when we ⁵ **have woken up / woke up** this morning, the view ⁶ **was / has been** incredible.
> I ⁷ **have never seen / never saw** anything so beautiful. We ⁸ **have left / left** the hotel at 10 am and we ⁹ **have been / were** very busy ¹⁰ **for / since** then! In the morning, we ¹¹ **have visited / visited** the Blue Mosque. After lunch we ¹² **have crossed / crossed** the Bosphorus on a ferry to visit the Asian side of the city. We ¹³ **haven't had / didn't have** anything to eat ¹⁴ **for / since** lunchtime. It's 9 pm and I'm really hungry! It's time for supper!
> Bye for now,

Your turn

5 Ask and answer with a partner. Choose one of the phrases in box A. Continue the conversations using phrases in box B.

A

> set off on a journey very early   visit a really big city
> go on a school trip   go to a theme park

B

> When did you go?   What did you do?
> Who did you go with?   Where did you go?
> What did you eat?   Did you like it?

A: Have you ever set off … ?
B: Yes, I have.
A: Where did you go?
B: I went to …

Discover Culture

1 Look at the photos. Do you know what they are?

2 Work with a partner. What do you know about Australia? Make a list of other images you might see in the video.

Find out about Australia.

Discovery EDUCATION

4.2 The strange and beautiful land of Australia

3 ▶ 4.2 Watch the video. Which images did you see in Exercise 1? Make a list of the other things that you saw under the categories below.
   1 famous places   2 animals   3 sports

4 ▶ 4.2 Watch the video again. Complete the sentences with the correct words.
   1 Uluru is a giant .... near Sydney.
   2 People first brought .... to Australia in the .....
   3 In the national park you can see ...., ... and wombats.
   4 .... shearing is popular all over the country.
   5 Cane .... are poisonous.
   6 Australian rules football is very similar to .....

5 Match these adjectives with the things that they describe in the video.

   confusing   unusual   famous   poisonous

   1 Uluru   3 toads
   2 camel-racing   4 Australian rules football

6 ▶ 4.2 What other information did you hear about these things? Watch the video again and check your answers.

   Millions of people travel to Australia every year.

7 What is the video about? Choose the best summary.
   a unusual things in Australia
   b well-known things about Australia
   c well-known and unusual things in Australia

Your turn

8 Ask and answer the questions with your partner.
   1 Would you like to go to Australia? Why/Why not?
   2 What landmarks, animals and sports are special to your own country?

Reading A poster presentation

1 Work with a partner. Look at the photos of New Zealand. What do you think life is like there?

2 🔊 1.49 Read the presentation. Whose culture and customs are important in New Zealand?

3 Read the presentation again. Match the headings with the correct paragraphs.
   A Education   D New Zealand identity
   B Art   E The perfect view
   C Getting active

Explore interesting adjectives

4 Complete the sentences with the adjectives from the text.
   1 an *important* part of New Zealand's identity
   2 has .... landscapes
   3 their .... *haka*
   4 Cricket is incredibly ....
   5 One of the most .... art forms

5 Use the adjectives from Exercise 4 to describe your own country.
   Football/Skiing is an important sport ...
   ➔ Vocabulary Bank • page 110

Your turn

6 Make notes about another country.
   1 What are the people and landscape like?
   2 What do you know about their sports and art?
   3 Do you know anything about their education system?

   The people are very friendly and the landscape is beautiful. I know they like football a lot. Many famous artists come from here. I don't really know much about the education system.

7 Ask and answer the questions from Exercise 6 with your partner. Ask him/her if he/she can help you to collect more information.

   Do you know anything about the education system in Spain?

New Zealand

1 *D New Zealand identity*
The first people to arrive about 1,000 years ago were from Eastern Polynesia. Their culture and their customs developed into the Maori way of life – this has been an important part of New Zealand's identity ever since.

2 ....
New Zealand has amazing landscapes with high mountains and over 3,800 lakes! There are at least twelve active volcanoes. The largest lake in New Zealand, Lake Taupo, lies in the crater of one of the biggest volcanoes on Earth. More than 30% of New Zealand is forest.

3 ....
New Zealanders love sports. The most famous sport is rugby – the All Blacks are famous for their spectacular haka, the Maori challenge dance before their international matches. Cricket is also incredibly popular. With 6,000 kilometres of coastline it also means water sports are very popular – sailing, kayaking, diving and surfing.

4 ....
One of the most striking art forms in Maori culture is the Ta moko, Maori tattoos. The design is incredibly complicated and they are made by tapping the needle into the skin. Maori men often have Ta moko on their faces and Maori women have them on their lips and chins.

5 ....
New Zealanders have to go to school from the age of six until they are 16. The school year starts in January or February and finishes in the middle of December. There are four terms with two-week holidays between each term. The school day starts at nine o'clock and finishes at three o'clock.

FACT! *The human population of New Zealand is 4 million. The sheep population is 36 million.*

UNIT 4

Speaking Signing up for an activity

Real talk: What's the most exciting thing you've ever done?

1. ▶ **4.3** Watch the teenagers in the video. What activities do they talk about?
   - river rafting
   - canyoning
   - skiing
   - walking behind a waterfall
   - jumping into water
   - sailing
   - playing in a concert
   - going on a rollercoaster

2. 💬 What's the most exciting thing *you've* ever done?

3. 🔊 **1.50** Listen to Gemma talking to an activity guide. What is she going to do?

4. Complete the conversation with the useful language.

   ### Useful language
   Where can I sign up?
   Can I ask you a few things about (…)?
   What about … ?
   What do I need to bring?
   How long is … ?
   Does the price include (…)?

5. 🔊 **1.50** Listen again and check your answers.

6. 💬 Work with a partner. Practise the conversation in Exercise 4.

7. 💬 Change the words in bold in the conversation. Use the ideas below. Take turns to ask and answer the questions.

Gemma:	Can I ¹ *ask you* a few things about the **canyoning trip**?
Guide:	The **Blue Canyon** one? Sure. What would you like to know?
Gemma:	Well, is it only for people who've already done it?
Guide:	No, you don't need any experience. We give training with qualified guides, and the **Blue Canyon** is fine for **beginners**.
Gemma:	Great! ²… need to bring? I haven't got a wetsuit or anything.
Guide:	That's OK. We provide a **wetsuit, helmet, shoes and life jacket**. Just bring **your swimsuit** and **towel** and some **warm clothes for after**.
Gemma:	OK, good! How ³… is the trip to **Blue Canyon**?
Guide:	It's **all day**, from **nine until six**.
Gemma:	I see. ⁴… **food**, then? Does the price ⁵… ?
Guide:	**Food is included** in the price. We look after everything, so you just enjoy the adventure!
Gemma:	Wow! It sounds fantastic. Where ⁶… sign up?
Guide:	Right here!

REGIS RIVER RAFTING
Whitewater rafting with qualified instructors
We provide: wetsuit, life jacket and helmet, hot drinks
You bring: swimsuit and towel, warm clothes
From beginners to advanced
Morning (9–12) or afternoon (3–6)

REGIS

TREKKING TOURS
Trekking with qualified instructors
We provide: maps, picnic lunch, transport
You bring: boots, warm clothes, a camera
Everyone welcome
All day (10–5)

Writing A travel blog

1 Look at the photos and read Mitch's blog. Where is he on holiday?

Mitch's holiday blog: Highway 101 Road Trip

What an amazing holiday! We've been on the road in our camper van for ten days, and since we left LA we've driven over 700 km, so we've already done half the trip. I had an extra waffle for breakfast to celebrate! Definitely my favourite place up to now has been Hearst Castle – what incredible buildings!

Today was another fantastic drive up the coast from Santa Cruz (where we stayed the night) to San Francisco. I've seen lots of pictures of the Golden Gate Bridge so I was very excited but … we didn't cross it!! Mum says it's on the *other* side of San Francisco so I haven't seen it yet. What a big disappointment!

Bye till tomorrow.

2 Read the blog again and answer the questions.
1. How many days has he been travelling?
2. How far has he travelled?
3. What places has he visited?
4. What has been his favourite place?
5. What has/hasn't he seen?

Useful language

Expressing how you feel, good or bad.
Use interesting activities to write about how you feel.
- What an *amazing* holiday! (or What a holiday!)
- What *incredible* buildings!

3 Look at the Useful language box. Find one example of how Mitch feels bad in the blog.

4 Complete the exclamations using the nouns (1–6) and a good (☺) or bad (☹) adjective from the box.

> beautiful   boring   comfortable   delicious   exciting   ugly

1. waffles ☺
   What delicious waffles!
2. trip ☹
   What a boring trip!
3. film ☺
4. beds ☺
5. building ☹
6. photos ☺

Get writing

PLAN

5 Make notes about a holiday blog post. Include information from Exercise 2 to help you.

WRITE

6 Write your holiday blog post. Use your notes and the model text to help you.

CHECK

7 Can you say YES to these questions?
- Is the information from Exercise 2 in your blog post?
- Have you included one or two exclamations to say how you feel?

3-4 Review

Vocabulary

1 Complete the sentences with the words in the box.

| buskers   ~~graffiti~~   exhibition |
| sculptures   living statue   concert hall |

1. There's some amazing _graffiti_ on the wall outside the library.
2. We often go to our local .... to hear classical music or opera.
3. I love .... that are made of stone or metal.
4. Did you see those ....? They're playing music in the park.
5. I went to an .... of modern art yesterday.
6. Have you seen the .... in the main square? You give him some money and he moves!

2 Write the names of the musical instruments.

1. saxophone

3 Complete the sentences with the phrases in the box and the correct form of *go*, *go on* or *go to*.

| ~~climbing~~   sailing   a safari   a guided tour |
| a summer camp   trekking |

1. We _go climbing_ every summer in the mountains.
2. They .... when they were in Italy. They walked 20 km a day.
3. I love .... – you can make new friends and learn new skills.
4. Jim is .... of Cambridge tomorrow. An expert takes you round and tells you the history of the city.
5. Do you want to .... at the weekend? It's very relaxing on the boat.
6. I'd love to .... and see wild animals, but it's very expensive.

4 Choose the correct word.

1. When did they come (back)/ up from their trip?
2. I picked out / up a bit of Italian on holiday.
3. They want to set up / off early in the morning.
4. I usually chill up / out in front of the TV at the weekend.
5. Where can we find out / off about day trips?
6. Let's look out / around the town while we're waiting.

Explore vocabulary

5 Complete the sentences with the words in the box. Use the correct form when necessary.

| dress up   post online   show up   take it in turns |
| first taste   keep watch   ~~make money~~   disabled |

1. I drew portraits at the school fair and I _made_ a lot of _money_.
2. When I was on the summer camp, I had my .... of climbing.
3. Kate .... late to the party. She missed the bus.
4. Can you .... those photos .... so I can see them?
5. What costume are you .... in to go to the party?
6. My little brothers always argue over toys, they can't .... to play with something.
7. When we went on a safari the guide .... at night for wild animals.
8. The theme park is great for .... people too – there aren't any steps and there's extra help if you need it.

6 Complete the text with the words in the box.

| ~~perfect~~   pick up   passionate about |
| take photos   amazing   cool stuff |
| popular   important |

Ireland is the ¹_perfect_ place to take a holiday. There is lots of ² .... to do for everyone like trekking in the ³ .... countryside or visiting the beautiful cities of Dublin or Cork. Music is an ⁴ .... part of Irish identity and the Irish are ⁵ .... music and dance. You can see traditional music played in places all over Dublin. There are lots of opportunities to ⁶ ...., for example the Giant's Causeway – it is incredibly ⁷ .... with photographers and tourists. Many people in Ireland speak Irish, but if you think you will ⁸ .... a little Irish, think again – it's very hard!

UNIT 3–4

Language focus

1 Complete the email with the verbs in the box. Use the present perfect.

| see | go | record | ~~visit~~ | not go | buy | take |

New mail +1

Hi Janice,
We're having a lovely time here in Paris. We ¹ *have visited* five art galleries and two museums. I ² .... never .... such wonderful art! We ³ .... to several lectures about modern art. I ⁴ .... them for you so you can listen later! Tony ⁵ .... hundreds of photos and he ⁶ .... a lot of posters and postcards! We ⁷ .... to the Picasso Museum – that's tomorrow.
See you soon,
Angie

2 Complete the conversation with the present perfect and *ever* or *never*. Use the verbs in brackets.

Mike:	This music is from South Africa. ¹ *have* you *ever heard* (hear) this kind of music?
Kevin:	Yes, I have. There's a concert tomorrow. ² .... you .... (go) to a concert of African music?
Mike:	No, I ³ .... (go) to a live concert.
Kevin:	Can you play any musical instruments?
Mike:	I can play the piano and my brother plays the guitar.
Kevin:	⁴ .... he .... (play) in any concerts?
Mike:	Yes, but I ⁵ .... (see) him play.

3 Complete the sentences with *for* or *since*.
1 I haven't seen Jim *for* a long time.
2 I've lived here .... a year.
3 I've picked up a lot of Spanish .... January.
4 We haven't had any homework .... Monday.
5 She's been in bed .... ten days – she's very ill.
6 She hasn't visited her friend .... weeks.

4 Complete the conversations with the verbs in brackets. Use the present perfect or past simple.
1 A: ¹ *Have you been* (be) to New York?
   B: Yes, we ² .... (go) there last year.
2 A: How long ³ .... Sarah .... (live) in Rome?
   B: She ⁴ .... (move) there six months ago.
3 A: What time ⁵ .... you .... (arrive)?
   B: We ⁶ .... (not be) here for very long – about ten minutes.

Language builder

5 Choose the correct words to complete the text.

Hi Keira!

How are you? I ¹ *a* this email to you in the hotel café in Prague – we've ² .... got back from the main square. We ³ .... here ⁴ .... two days and we have ⁵ .... quite a lot. My Dad ⁶ .... lots of photos and he takes ages so we always ⁷ .... wait for him. Yesterday while we ⁸ .... for my Dad, we ⁹ .... some ice cream in a really cool art café. Prague is a beautiful city – you ¹⁰ .... come here some time! OK, Mum and Sam are back – we haven't had dinner ¹¹ .....
Talk later!

Fiona

1	a am writing	b write	c have written
2	a yet	b just	c already
3	a have been	b are	c have gone
4	a since	b for	c just
5	a already seen	b yet seen	c seen already
6	a took	b takes usually	c usually takes
7	a should	b must	c have to
8	a have waited	b were waiting	c waited
9	a had	b have had	c were having
10	a should	b have	c mustn't
11	a just	b already	c yet

Speaking

6 Match the sentences.
1 Shall I ask my mum to get us? *b*
2 How long is the trip?
3 What do I need to bring?
4 What time shall we meet?
5 Where can I sign up?
6 Do you fancy going to a concert?

a It starts at 8 pm, so how about 7.30?
b Yes, that's a good idea.
c Yeah, why not?
d A towel and a swimming costume.
e It's all morning.
f Right here!

Say it right!

Unit 1 /ɪ/ and /iː/

1 🔊 1.06 **Listen and repeat.**
/ɪ/ wind   city   /iː/ freeze   beach

2 🔊 1.07 **Listen and choose.**

/iː/	/ɪ:/
1 it	eat
2 live	leave
3 hit	heat
4 ship	sheep
5 fill	feel

3 Match the words to the correct sound.

> ~~extreme~~   free   heat   give   listen
> six   swim   teach

/ɪ/ *give*   /iː/ *extreme*

4 🔊 1.08 **Listen, check and repeat.**

Unit 2 Word stress

1 🔊 1.22 **Listen and repeat.**

> orchestra   invention   microphone   tomorrow
> Internet   computer   important   instrument

2 🔊 1.23 Listen again and match the words to the correct stress pattern.

•orchestra	in•vention

3 🔊 1.23 **Listen, check and repeat.**

4 Add the words to the chart.

> develop   concentrate   exercise   creative
> Saturday   correctly

5 🔊 1.24 **Listen, check and repeat.**

Unit 3 Strong and weak forms of *have*

1 🔊 1.35 **Listen and repeat.**
1 **Have** you ever been to Rome?
2 Yes, I **have**.
3 I**'ve** seen the film, but I **haven't** read the book.

2 🔊 1.36 **Listen to the conversations. Are the forms of *have* strong or weak?**

1 A: ¹**Have** you ever eaten shark?
   B: Shark? No, I ²**haven't**.
   A: Well, ³I**'ve** tried it and it's delicious. What about jellyfish? ⁴**Have** you tried that?
   B: Yes, I ⁵**have**.
   A: I ⁶**haven't** tried it, but it sounds horrible!

2 A: ¹I**'ve** just finished reading *The Hunger Games*. ²**Have** you ever read it?
   B: No, I ³**haven't**. Are those books good?
   A: Yes! ⁴**Have** you seen the films?
   B: Yes, I ⁵**have**, but ⁶I**'ve** only seen the first film.

3 🔊 1.36 **Listen, check and repeat.**

4 Work with a partner. Practise the conversations in Exercise 2.

Unit 4 Consonant to vowel linking

1 🔊 1.46 **Listen and repeat.**
1 The school day starts at eight o'clock.
2 We set off early in the morning.

2 🔊 1.47 **Listen and mark the links between consonant and vowel sounds.**
1 We visited a big city. (1 link)
2 Did you find out what happened at the party? (2 links)
3 Let's look around the town after lunch. (2 links)
4 Chill out! The exam isn't until Friday. (3 links)
5 How do you chill out? (1 link)
6 What languages are easy to pick up? (2 links)

3 🔊 1.47 **Listen, check and repeat.**

Grammar reference

Starter Unit

Wh- questions

- We usually make questions by changing the word order. We put the auxiliary verb before the subject.
  Where do you live?
- In present simple questions we use *do/does*.
  What time does the film start?
- In past simple questions we use *did*.
  How did you do in your exam?
- We don't use *do/does/did* in questions when *who/what/which* is the subject of the sentence.
  Who texted Ben? (subject)
  Who did Ben text? (object)

Comparatives and superlatives

	Comparative	Superlative
1 or 2 syllable Adjectives	adjective + -er / -ier	(the) adjective + -est / -iest
	old – old**er**	old – the old**est**
	happy – happ**ier**	happy – the happ**iest**
3 or more syllables	more + adjective **more** interesting	(the) most + adjective the **most** interesting
Irregular forms *good* and *bad*	good – **better**	good – the **best**
	bad – **worse**	bad – the **worst**

- We use comparative and superlative forms to compare things. To make comparative forms we add *-er* to 1 and 2 syllable adjectives. When the adjective ends in *-y*, we change it to an *-i*.
  My dad's tall but my uncle is taller.
  Kelly's friendly but Sam's friendlier.

Adjectives and adverbs

quiet	quietly	bad	badly
happy	happily	easy	easily
sad	sadly	quick	quickly
good	well	careful	carefully

- Adjectives tell us about a noun. We use adjectives before nouns and after some verbs, especially *be*.
  Alice is a good student.
  Please be quiet.
- Adverbs tell us about verbs. An adverb tells us how somebody does something or how something happens.
  Jack painted the picture carefully.
  Please speak quietly.

Comparative and superlative adverbs

- In general, comparative and superlative forms of adverbs are the same as for adjectives. With adverbs ending in *-ly*, we use *more* for the comparative and *most* for the superlative:

Adverb	Comparative	Superlative
quiet**ly**	**more** quietly	**most** quietly
slow**ly**	**more** slowly	**most** slowly
serious**ly**	**more** seriously	**most** seriously

Could you talk more quietly? ~~Could you talk quietlier?~~
The teacher spoke more slowly.

- Some adverbs have irregular comparative forms.

Adverb	Comparative	Superlative
badly	worse	worst
far	farther/further	farthest/furthest
little	less	least
well	better	best

You're driving worse today than yesterday.
The girl ran further than the boy.

Past simple

- We use the past simple to talk about completed events and actions in the past. We form regular past tense forms by adding *-ed*.
  I played football yesterday.
  I walked to school this morning.
- We form the negative of the past simple with subject + *didn't* + infinitive.
  I didn't go the cinema.
- We form past simple questions with *did* + subject + infinitive.
  Did she enjoy the party? Yes, she did.
- We form *Wh-* question in the past simple with Question word + *did* + subject + infinitive.
  What did you do on holiday?
- Some verbs are irregular in the past simple. They don't follow any pattern. (See irregular verbs list on page 126.)
- *Was* and *were* are the past simple forms of *be*.
  He was in town for two hours.
- To form *Yes/No* questions, we use *was/were* before the subject. We don't use *do*.
  Was he happy? Were the cats eating?
- To form *Wh-* questions, we put the question word before *was/were*.
  What film was it?
  When were you at the park?

Grammar reference

Unit 1

Present simple vs. present continuous

- We use the present simple to talk about facts, habits and routines.
  My sister likes cold weather.
  I go to school early every day.
  He doesn't like fish.
  We don't live in Malaga.
  Do you live in France?
  Where does she live?
- We use the present continuous to talk about actions in progress at the time of speaking or around that time.
  Silvia is driving to work this week.
  I'm working on my school project at the moment.
- We form the affirmative with subject + be + verb + -ing.
  I'm reading.
  They're listening.
- We form the negative with *be not* + verb + -ing. *Not* is usually contracted.
  You aren't listening.
  She isn't sleeping.
- We form questions, with *be* + subject + verb + -ing.
  Is Ana doing her homework?
- In information questions, we put the *Wh-* question word before *be*.
  Where are they shopping?
  What book is he reading?

1 Complete the conversation. Use the present simple or the present continuous form of the verbs in brackets.

John:	Hello. ¹…. (you do) anything at the moment?
Katie:	Right now, I ²…. (look after) my brother. Why?
John:	What time ³…. (your mum get) home?
Katie:	She ⁴…. (work) late every Thursday, so at about half past seven. Why?
John:	They ⁵…. (show) that new comedy film at the cinema in town. It ⁶…. (start) at half past eight. My sister and I ⁷…. (think) about going. ⁸…. (you want) to come with us?
Katie:	Yes, please! Let's meet at the cinema at eight!

Adverbs of frequency

never   hardly ever   sometimes   usually   often   always

- We use adverbs of frequency to say how often something happens.
- We put them before the main verb but after the verb *to be*.
  It hardly ever snows here.
  There are often snowstorms here in winter.
- *Often*, *sometimes* and *usually* can also come at the beginning of the sentence.
  Sometimes, my family and I have barbecues.
- We use adverbs of frequency (*always, often, hardly ever …*) with the present simple. We use *at the moment* and *now* with the present continuous.
  My dad often plays computer games with me.
  My mum is running at the moment.

2 Put the words in the correct order to make sentences.

1. washes / the / Theo / never / car *Theo never washes the car.*
2. hardly / watch / TV / They / ever
3. late / sometimes / am / school / for / I
4. get / marks / exams / good / You / always / in
5. on / play / usually / We / football / Wednesdays
6. homework / with / often / She / helps me / my

Past simple vs. past continuous

* See Starter Unit for past simple.

- We use the past continuous to talk about actions in progress at a certain time in the past.
  At lunchtime, it was raining.
- We form affirmative sentences with subject + *was/were* + verb + -ing.
  He was crying.
  We weren't listening.
- We form the negative with *was/were* + *not* (*n't*) + verb + -ing. *Not* is usually contracted.
  They weren't helping to tidy.

3 Complete the text. Use the past simple or the past continuous form of the verbs in brackets.

When I woke up, it ¹ *was raining* (rain). I ²…. (walk) to the bathroom, but my brother ³…. (have) a shower. I ⁴…. (tell) him to be quick and then I ⁵…. (go) to the kitchen. Dad ⁶…. (read) the newspaper, and Mum ⁷…. (listen) to the news.' ⁸…. (you sleep) well?' asked Dad. 'No,' I said, 'I ⁹…. (have) a very strange dream about a horse in my English class!

Grammar reference   99

Grammar reference

Unit 2

should

+	I/You/He/She/It/We/You/They	should	help.
–	I/You/He/She/It/We/You/They	shouldn't	
?	Should		help?
+	Yes,	I/you/he/she/it/we/you/they	should.
+	No,		shouldn't.

- We use *should* to say what we think is a good idea, or important to do.
  You should organise a party for your birthday.
  They should ask the teacher.
- *Should* is the same in all forms.
- We use an infinitive without *to* after *should*.
  John should ~~to~~ get more sleep.

1 Complete the questions and sentences with the correct form of *should* and the verbs in the box.

> invite ~~try~~ not play listen wear not talk

1 You *should try* harder – you can do it!
2 She .... her music loudly.
3 What .... I .... to the party?
4 They .... in here – it's a library.
5 .... we .... Leo to the cinema with us?
6 He .... to the teacher in class.

must

+	I/You/He/She/It/We/You/They	must	go.
–		mustn't	
?	Must		go?
+	Yes,	I/you/he/she/it/we/you/they	must.
–	No,		mustn't.

- We use *must* to say what we think is necessary to do.
  You must listen to this song. It's fantastic!
- We use *mustn't* to say what we think is necessary not to do.
  We mustn't forget to buy her a present.
- *Must* is the same in all forms.
- We use the infinitive without *to* after *must*.
  You must remember that story. (~~You must to remember that story.~~)

2 Choose the correct words.

1 You **should / mustn't** forget to call me tonight.
2 Students **should / mustn't** run in the corridors.
3 You **must / shouldn't** stay up so late – you're tired today.
4 I think they **must / should** relax more.
5 We **shouldn't / mustn't** be noisy in the library.

have to/don't have to

+	I/We/You/They	have to	practise.
	He/She/It	has to	
–	I/We/You/They	don't have to	
	He/She/It	doesn't have to	
?	Do	I/we/you/they	have to practise.
	Does	he/she/it	
+	Yes,	I/we/you/they	do.
		he/she/it	does.
–	No,	I/we/you/they	don't.
		he/she/it	doesn't.

- We use *have to* to say what is necessary to do.
  You have to answer all the questions in the exam.
  Toby has to look after his sister this afternoon.
- We use *don't have to* to say what isn't necessary to do, but is an option or a choice.
  I don't have to help you with the homework.
  Elsie doesn't have to get up early tomorrow.
- Question words go at the beginning of the question.
  How much homework do you have to do?
  When do we have to make a decision?

3 Complete the sentences and questions with the correct form of *have to*.

1 You *don't have to* phone. You can email for information.
2 At my school, we .... play hockey, but there is a school team.
3 Doctors .... study for seven or eight years.
4 Why .... she .... do the exam again?
5 .... we .... bring our instruments with us?

4 Complete the sentences with *don't have to*, *doesn't have to* or *mustn't*.

1 He *doesn't have to* get up early tomorrow.
2 He .... eat in here – it isn't allowed.
3 I .... give this to the teacher until Friday.
4 She .... use those scissors – they're dangerous.
5 You .... forget to feed the cat.

Grammar reference

Unit 3

Present perfect for indefinite past time

+	I/We/You/They	have passed	the exam.
	He/She/It	has passed	
-	I/We/You/They	haven't passed	
	He/She/It	hasn't passed	
?	Have	I/we/you/they	passed the exam?
	Has	he/she/it	
+ Yes,		I/we/you/they	have.
		he/she/it	has.
- No,		I/we/you/they	haven't.
		he/she/it	hasn't.

- We use the present perfect to talk about experiences and facts in the past when the exact time is not mentioned or important.
  The school have organised a trip to Germany.
  I've seen some fantastic graffiti.
- We form the affirmative with subject + *have/has* + past participle.
  I've bought tickets for the exhibition.
  She's given me some good advice.
- We form the negative with subject + *haven't/hasn't* + past participle.
  Max hasn't seen the mural.
  They haven't asked me for help.
- Regular past participles end in *-ed*, *-d* or *-ied*.
  want–wanted   believe–believed
  play–played   worry–worried
- Many common verbs have irregular past participles.
  go–gone   put–put
  see–seen   hear–heard
- We use *be* (*been*) to say somebody has returned from a place or from doing an activity.
- We use *go* (*gone*) to say somebody has not returned from a place or from doing an activity.
  He's gone shopping. (He is at the shop now.)
  He's been shopping. (He has returned.)

1 Complete the sentences. Use the present perfect form of the verbs in brackets.

1. I *'ve finished* washing the car. (finish)
2. We …. so many great paintings today. (see)
3. Your postcard from Tom …. (not arrive)
4. You …. a letter to your aunty. (not write)
5. They …. visiting the museums. (enjoy)
6. She …. to Leo four times this week. (speak)

Present perfect with *ever/never*

?	Have	I/we/you/they	ever	seen	the film?
	Has	he/she/it			
+	I/We/You/They	have		never	the film.
	He/She/It	has			

- We often use *ever* in present perfect questions when the exact time isn't important.
  Has she ever had piano lessons?
  Have you every broken your arm or leg?
- We often use *never* to say not at any time when answering these questions.
  He's never met anybody famous.
  I've never lived in another city. I've only ever lived here.

2 Look at the table. Write present perfect questions with *ever*. Then write the correct answers.

	Charlotte	Aiden and Milo	You
climb a mountain	1 ✓	5 ✗	9 ?
win a prize	2 ✗	6 ✓	10 ?
go to a music festival	3 ✗	7 ✓	11 ?
make a cake	4 ✓	8 ✗	12 ?

1 *Has Charlotte ever climbed a mountain? Yes, she has.*

3 Complete the conversation. Use the present perfect form of the verbs in brackets.

A: [1] *Have* you *heard* (hear) the new Kaiser Chiefs CD?
B: No, I [2] …. . I prefer pop music.
A: Oh! What bands [3] …. you …. (see) in concert?
B: I [4] …. (never see) a band in concert. I don't like loud noise and lots of people.
A: I love it! I [5] …. (be) to lots of concerts. [6] …. you …. (ever be) to the small concerts in town?
B: No, I [7] …. .
A: I [8] …. (buy) two tickets to see a new band this weekend. Do you want to come?
B: Maybe. I [9] …. (not finish) my homework and my mum [10] …. (ask) me to help her too.
A: Come on!
B: OK!

Grammar reference

Unit 4

Present perfect with *still, yet, already* and *just*

- We often use *still, yet, already* and *just* with the present perfect.
  Jack's already been to Australia three times.
  I haven't had time to go shopping yet.
  We still haven't decided where to go on holiday.
  Dad's just got home and he's feeling tired.
- We use *still* with negative verbs to express that something we expected has not happened, but imagine it will happen in the future. We put *still* directly after the subject.
  My uncle still hasn't telephoned.
- We use *yet* with negative verbs to emphasise that something we expected has not happened. We put *yet* after the complete verb phrase.
  John hasn't arrived yet.
- We use *yet* in questions to ask about things we don't think have happened.
  Have you bought the train tickets yet?
- We use *already* to explain that something happened before we expected or to emphasise it has happened. We usually put *already* between *have* and the past participle.
- We use *just* with the present perfect to talk about very recent events and actions.
  I've just heard the good news. It's fantastic!

1 Complete the sentences with *still, yet, already* or *just*.

1. You ...*still*... haven't bought me a birthday present.
2. I haven't seen the *Superman* film ..... .
3. Harry's .... broken his new computer.
4. They haven't asked their parents .... .
5. I've .... had some juice.
6. Lucy .... hasn't decided what she wants to do at university.

2 Complete the sentences. Use the present perfect with *still, yet, already* or *just* and the phrases in the box.

> not eat   have some juice   start   see   not hear

1. Do you want a drink?
   No, thanks. I've *just had some juice*.
2. What do you think of the news?
   I don't know. I ..... .
3. Do you want to watch this DVD?
   Not really. I .... it.
4. Do the children want some sweets?
   No, they .... their dinner .... .
5. Sorry, I'm late.
   It's OK. We .... .

Present perfect with *for* and *since*

- We use *for* and *since* with the present perfect to say how long something has been true.
  I've lived here since I was seven.
  She hasn't gone climbing for three years.
- We use *for* with periods of time.
  My parents have been married for twenty-one years.
- We use *since* with a reference to a specific time.
  I've known her since 2009.
  Emma and Anna haven't spoken since the party.

3 Complete the table with the words in the box.

> ~~three weeks~~   Monday   2008   a long time
> two hours   last December   this morning
> months   twelve weeks

for	since
three weeks	

Present perfect vs. past simple

- We use the past simple when the moment in which something happened has ended. When it happened isn't always mentioned, usually because it is clear.
  I went to Liverpool in June. (It's now July.)
- We use the present perfect when something started or happened in the past and continues to be true. We can say how long something has been true, but not when it started.
  I've been to Liverpool. (When isn't specified, but continues to be true.)
  They've begun the exam. (The exam hasn't finished.)

4 Complete the conversation. Use the present perfect or the past simple form of the verbs in brackets.

Mum:	Sam, [1] ...*Have you seen*... (you/see) Julia?
Sam:	No, I [2] .... (not see) her since last night. We [3] .... (watch) TV but she was tired, so she [4] .... (go) to bed. Why?
Mum:	She isn't here and she [5] .... (go) to school. Her teacher [6] .... (just call).
Sam:	I don't know. [7] .... (you ask) Dad?
Mum:	I rang the office, but he [8] .... (still not reply) to my message.
Julia:	Hi!
Mum:	Julia! Where [9] .... (you be)?
Julia:	Sorry, Mum. I [10] .... (not feel) very well, so I [11] .... (go) to the doctor.

Vocabulary Bank

UNIT 1

Jog your memory!

1 Cover the rest of the page. How many words to describe extreme weather and survival essentials can you remember?

Extreme weather (page 9)

boiling	heavy rain
freezing	high winds
hail	snowstorm
heatwave	thunder and lightning

1 Look at the words in the box. Write sentences about when you have experienced these weather conditions.
I went on holiday to Spain last year. It was boiling.

2 Work with a partner. Talk about your sentences. Where were you and what was the weather like?

Survival essentials (page 12)

sun cream	map	first aid kit
water bottle	sleeping bag	camera
sunglasses	penknife	glasses
compass	torch	contact lenses

1 Look at the words in the box. What do you pack when you go on holiday?

2 Add three more items that you usually pack to the list.

Explore prepositional phrases (page 15)

| a ship | the Internet | the planet |
| both directions | the island | |

1 Look at the words in the box. Write the words in the correct column.

in	on
	a ship

2 Add these words to the correct column.

| October | South Africa | the middle |
| television | total | Earth |

hail – granizar

Study tip

Keep a record of all your new words. You can write a translation or a definition in your vocabulary notebook or on cards.

Vocabulary Bank 107

Vocabulary Bank

Jog your memory!

1 Cover the rest of the page. How many words to describe priorities and performing can you remember?

Priorities (page 19)

chat with	around the house
do	for yourself
do	enough sleep
get	friends online
hang out	something creative
have time	sports
help	with friends

1 Turn to page 19. Look at the words for two minutes.

2 Can you remember them all? Match the words in the box to make expressions.

Performing (page 22)

act	on stage
dancing	orchestra
instruments	play (the piano)
microphone	voice

1 Look at the words in the box. Which things do you need to have lessons for?

2 Which words are verbs and which words are nouns?
act – verb

Explore verb + noun collocations (page 20)

catch a cold	have a snack
concentrate in your lessons	surf the Internet
get more sleep	watch TV

1 Look at the words in the box. Talk to your partner about when you do these activities or when they happen.
I always catch a cold in the winter.

2 Match the collocations from the text on page 20. Which collocation is a verb + adjective?

get out	relaxed
catch up	a good night's sleep
get	of bed
feel	on sleep

Explore prepositions (page 25)

between	near	over
in front of	of	until

1 Look at the words in the box. Write true and false sentences for you using the prepositions.
My house is near a river.

2 Work with a partner. Say your sentences and guess which sentences are true and which are false.

catch a cold (verb + noun)
feel relaxed (verb + adjective)

Study tip

Write collocations together and make a note of the form.

Vocabulary Bank

UNIT 3

🧠 Jog your memory!

1 Cover the rest of the page. How many words to describe art and instruments can you remember?

Art around us (page 31)

busker	living statue
concert hall	mural
exhibition	painting
gallery	portrait painter
graffiti	sculpture
juggler	

1 Look at the words in the box. Choose a word. Don't tell your partner. Describe the word. Can your partner guess what it is?
You can hear an orchestra play here.

Instruments (page 34)

banjo	flute	piano	violin
cello	guitar	recorder	trumpet
clarinet	keyboards	saxophone	tambourine
drums	mouth organ		

1 Look at the words in the box. Match them to the correct musical family. Which instrument doesn't fit into any family?

wind	string	percussion

2 Talk to your partner about instruments you play or have tried. Which is your favourite?

🔍 Explore collocations (page 32)

good at	post online
make money	take photos
passionate about	work hard

1 Look at the words in the box. Match them to the correct collocation pattern.

adjective + preposition	verb + noun	verb + adverb
good at		

2 Can you add three more words to the chart that collocate with any of the adjectives, prepositions, verbs or nouns?

🔍 Explore phrasal verbs with *up* (page 37)

dress up	pick up	tidy up
light up	set up	show up

1 Look at the words in the box. Write an example sentence for three of the phrasal verbs.
My mum always asks me to tidy up my bedroom.

2 Look at the verbs below. Which verb doesn't go with *up* to make a phrasal verb? Can you work out what the preposition is? Use a dictionary to check the meanings.

look	fall	give
set	add	catch
get	turn	grow

up	down
dress up	*get down*
show up	*turn down*

📖 Study tip

Write phrasal verbs in sets.

Vocabulary Bank

UNIT 4

Jog your memory!

1. Cover the rest of the page. How many expressions with *go* and phrasal verbs can you remember?

Expressions with *go* (page 41)

a guided tour	sailing
a safari	skiing
a school exchange	summer camp
a theme park	trekking
climbing	

1. Look at the words and phrases in the box. Match them with the correct heading.

go	go on	go to

2. Compare your list with your partner. Talk about which of the activities you like doing or have done.

   I go on a summer camp every year. I really enjoy it. We went trekking in the mountains last year.

Phrasal verbs (page 44)

chill	back
come	off
find	out
look	out
pick	round
set	up

1. Turn to page 44. Look at the phrasal verbs for one minute.

2. Can you remember them all? Match the words in the box to make phrasal verbs.

Explore interesting adjectives (page 47)

important	spectacular
amazing	popular
striking	

1. Look again at page 47. What additional adjective is used to describe the tattoos?

2. Write a sentence to show the meaning of each adjective.

   I have got some really important exams next week.

amaze (v) amazing (adj) amazingly (adv)

Study tip

Write other forms of words in your vocabulary notebook to help extend your vocabulary.

1 CLIL

Biology Global warming

1 Work with a partner. Answer the questions about the greenhouse effect.
1. What is the 'greenhouse effect'?
2. Which gases cause the greenhouse effect?
3. What is a greenhouse?
4. How does a greenhouse work?

2 Read the texts (a–d) and match the questions in Exercise 1.

3 🔊 1.51 Listen and check.

a A greenhouse is a structure made of glass or plastic. Farmers and gardeners use them for growing plants in.

b A greenhouse changes sunlight into heat. The Sun's radiation goes through the glass or plastic walls and roof as light. This heats up the air, then the walls and roof keep the heat inside.

c When we talk about the greenhouse effect, we mean the planet is working like a greenhouse. The Sun's **radiation** enters the Earth's atmosphere and heats up the Earth's surface. Thermal, **infra-red radiation** comes from the Earth's surface, but **gases** in the atmosphere don't allow it all to escape. In fact, they reflect it back at the Earth like the walls and roof of a greenhouse. This causes what scientists call 'global warming'.

d Different gases cause the greenhouse effect. The most common are water vapour, carbon dioxide (CO_2), methane, nitrous oxide and ozone. All of these gases exist naturally in our environment. Without them, the Earth would be too cold to support life – but too much of them can make temperatures rise. In fact, nowadays, the average global surface temperature is almost a degree higher than it was a hundred years ago.

4 Match the words in bold from the text to the numbers in the diagram.

5 Work with a partner. What problems does global warming cause? Make a list.

6 Read the information and check your answers from Exercise 5.

Higher temperatures are changing our environment. The Polar ice caps are melting and causing sea levels to rise. This produces floods in coastal areas and also affects ecosystems in the world's oceans and seas. It can cause extreme weather conditions, too – violent storms and hurricanes, for example. And it doesn't stop there. The higher temperatures make water evaporate from the land more quickly. This causes water loss and can turn good land into deserts. This desertification makes land more difficult to farm, and, of course, affects wildlife.

Your turn

7 Work with a partner. Make a list of things you can do at home to reduce the amount of CO_2 you produce. Then compare your list with another pair.

Learn about the greenhouse effect.
- Why is the Earth getting hotter?
- What happens to the oceans?
- What happens to the water?

Discovery EDUCATION

1.4 Hot topics

2 CLIL

P.E. Avoiding sports injuries

1 Work with a partner. Match the body parts to the words in the box.

> joints   muscles   ~~ligaments~~
> shoulder   ankle   knee

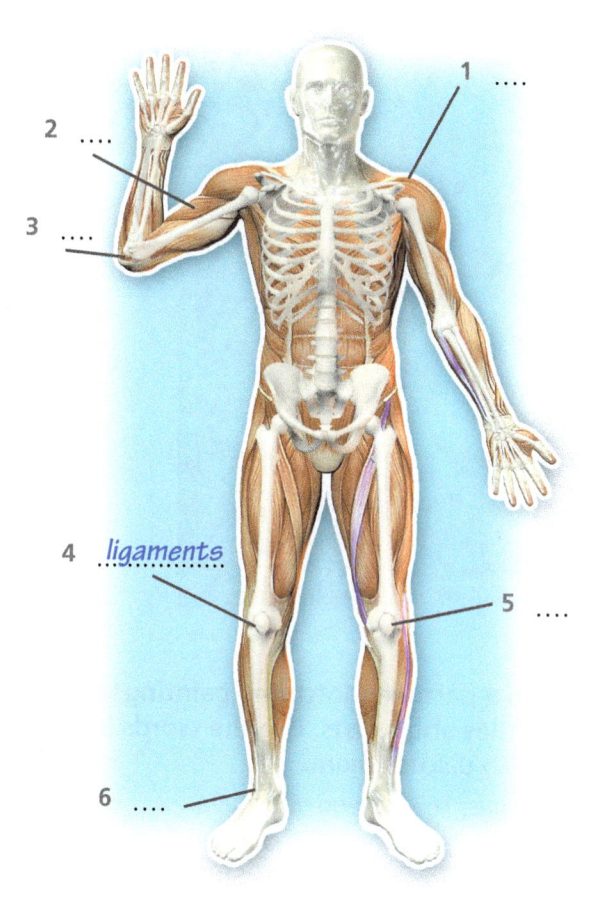

1 ....
2 ....
3 ....
4 ligaments
5 ....
6 ....

2 Complete the introduction giving advice on avoiding sports injuries with words from Exercise 1.

> Playing sports and taking exercise can be fun and can help you stay healthy, but anyone can get injured. Sports injuries can affect all parts of the body, but most injuries affect ¹...., ².... and ³..... Certain types of sport can affect different parts of the body. Tennis players often have ⁴... problems, for example, and people who go jogging can have problems with ⁵.... and ⁶.....

3 🔊 1.52 Listen and check.

4 🔊 1.53 Complete the advice with the words in the box. Then listen and check.

> injuries   ~~blood flow~~   stiff   pain   muscles   equipment

We can avoid most problems by following these simple guidelines.

1 Prepare properly for sport. Warm-up exercises before doing sport increase the ¹ _blood flow_ to the ².... and make them more flexible.

2 Cooling down is important, too. It stops you feeling ³.... the next day.

3 Get the right ⁴..... Using the wrong type of sports shoes or a tennis racquet of the wrong weight can cause problems.

4 Be careful with technique and posture. Talking to experienced sports people about this can help you avoid unnecessary ⁵.....

5 If you feel ⁶.... during exercise, it's a sign that there's a problem, so stop!

6 Don't start doing sport again too soon after an injury. Wait for the pain to go first. Doing sport too soon after an injury can make it worse.

Your turn

5 Work with a partner. Choose a sport. Make a leaflet explaining how to avoid injury in a sport.

Learn about helping someone.
- What does Bear Grylls do first?
- Why doesn't his mobile phone work?
- How does Bear pull Jesse up the mountain?

Discovery EDUCATION

2.4 Mountain rescue

3 CLIL

Art Perspective

1 Work with a partner. Look at the paintings. Can you see anything unusual about them?

2 🔊 1.54 Read the information about perspective. Check your ideas about the paintings.

> In the past, pictures of people, places and things didn't look like they do in real life. They looked flat and out of proportion. In the 13th century, artists began to produce life-like images by giving their pictures perspective.
>
> When we look at things around us, they are three dimensional (3D) – they have volume and depth. An artist uses perspective to create a representation on a two dimensional (2D) piece of paper or canvas of how we see things in real life with space, distance and depth between the various objects.
>
> Foreshortening objects gives the impression of perspective. The artist reduces the size of objects in a picture as they follow the viewer's line of sight into the distance. These lines converge in vanishing points on the viewer's horizon and the objects become too small to see. This makes parts of the image appear far away in the background or close to the viewer in the foreground.

3 Read the information again and answer the questions.
1. When did artists start to use perspective?
2. What were pictures like before that?
3. What does an artist use perspective for?
4. How does an artist show perspective?
5. What happens to objects close to the vanishing point?

4 🔊 1.55 Listen to a teacher and students in an art class. Which of the following do they mention?
- lines of sight
- shadow
- middle ground
- landscape
- vanishing point
- background
- three dimensional
- foreshortening

5 Work with a partner. Match the paintings with the titles and artists. Use the words in Exercise 4 to discuss them.
a *Las Meninas,* 1656, Diego Velázquez
b *Paris Street, Rainy day,* 1877, Gustave Caillebotte

Your turn

6 Choose a painting. Use the Internet to find out information about it.
Think about …
… who painted it and when.
… the use of perspective in the painting.
… what you like/don't like about the painting.
Share your ideas in class.

Learn about renaissance painters.
- Where did the renaissance begin?
- What did the renaissance painters want to do?
- Why did they want to do this?

Discovery EDUCATION

3.4 Art in perspective

4 CLIL

Geography Time zones

1 Work with a partner. Complete the diagram with the parallels and meridians (1–4).
1. The Equator
2. The Tropic of Cancer
3. The Tropic of Capricorn
4. The Prime/Greenwich Meridian

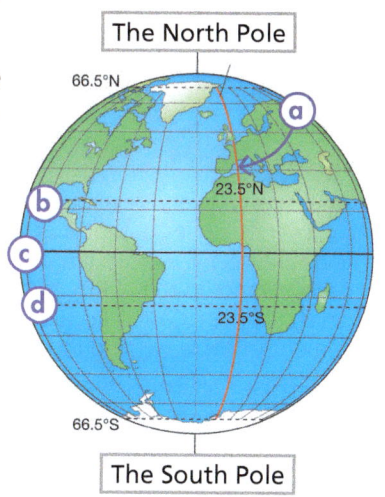

The North Pole
66.5°N
a
23.5°N
b
c
d
23.5°S
66.5°S
The South Pole

2 🔊 1.56 Read the information about parallels and meridians. Check your answers to Exercise 1.

THE EARTH AND ITS IMAGINARY LINES

Lines of latitude or parallels are horizontal lines dividing the Earth's surface. The line of latitude in the centre of the sphere is called the Equator. The Equator divides the globe into two hemispheres. Anything above the Equator is in the northern hemisphere and anything below is in the southern hemisphere.

Coordinates specify a north-south position on the Earth's surface, ranging from 0 degrees on the equator to 90 degrees at the poles. The North Pole is at 90 degrees north, and the South Pole is at 90 degrees south.

The Tropic of Cancer and The Tropic of Capricorn are two other important parallels. The Tropic of Cancer is above the Equator at 23.5 degrees north and the Tropic of Capricorn is below the Equator at 23.5 degrees south. These two lines of latitude mark the northern and southern limits of what is known as the tropics.

Lines of longitude or meridians are the vertical lines dividing the Earth's surface. The line of longitude passing through the Royal Observatory at Greenwich, near London, is the Prime Meridian. It's the international zero-longitude reference line. Places to the east of the Prime Meridian are in the eastern hemisphere, and places to the west are in the western hemisphere.

3 🔊 1.57 Complete the information about time zones with the words and phrases in the box. Then listen and check.

add   daylight   direction   forward
thirty   twenty-four

Time zones

There are ^{1}…. time zones in the world. Most of the time zones are one hour divisions, but a few are ^{2}…. or forty-five minutes.

Some higher latitude countries use ^{3}…. saving time. In the autumn, the clocks are put back, and in the spring the clocks are put ^{4}….

To calculate the time in a different time zone, you have to add or subtract hours depending on the ^{5}…. you are going. If you are going east, you need to ^{6}…. hours. If you are going west, you need to subtract them.

Your turn

4 Ask and answer with your partner.
1. What hemisphere do you live in?
2. Do you live closer to the Tropic of Cancer or the Tropic of Capricorn?
3. If you live in London and travel to New York, would you need to put your watch back or forward?

Learn about the world.
- What two different things can we use to look at the world?
- Where is Houston?
- Where is it always cold?

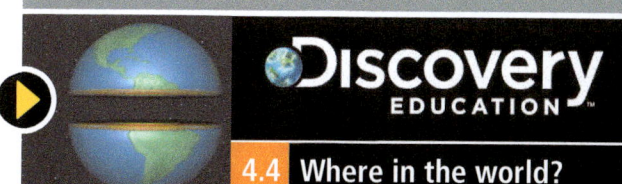

Discovery EDUCATION
4.4 Where in the world?

Project 1

An unusual hobby poster

PARKOUR
take to the streets!

WHAT IS IT?
Parkour comes from military training and involves running, jumping and climbing over obstacles outdoors. It can also involve moving on your hands and feet like a cat. It is a non-competitive activity which started in France in the 1980s and became popular through documentaries, films like *Casino Royale* (a James Bond movie) and TV advertisements. People who do the sport are called traceurs (for boys) or traceuses (for girls).

WHAT DO YOU NEED?
Nothing! You don't have to use any special equipment. Traceurs usually wear casual, sporty clothes like T-shirts, tracksuit bottoms and running shoes.

WHERE CAN YOU DO IT?
The best thing about parkour is that you can do it anywhere! Traceurs use urban and rural areas in places like parks, playgrounds, gyms and offices.

HOW CAN YOU DO IT?
Start by following the steps below:
1. Find somewhere safe like a park or a garden.
2. Practise running and jumping to help improve your balance.
3. Then try to jump backwards or do cartwheels (when you stand on your hands and land on your feet).
4. Finally, try to do this from a small height and land on the ground. And this is parkour!

Look

1 Read the poster. Answer the following questions.
1. Which actions does parkour involve?
2. When and where did it start?
3. How did it become popular?
4. What do traceurs wear?
5. Where can you do it?
6. Name two parkour movements from the text.

Prepare

2 Work in groups of three or four. Choose an unusual hobby that is popular with teenagers in your country. Use the Internet, books or magazines to find information about it. Find out about …
- where it comes from.
- what you need.
- where you can do it.
- how to do it.

3 Find photos or draw pictures of the activity. Make a poster with the photos and the information about it.

Present

4 In your groups present your poster to the rest of the class. Then ask them questions about the hobby. Can they remember all the important facts?

Project 2

A magazine article

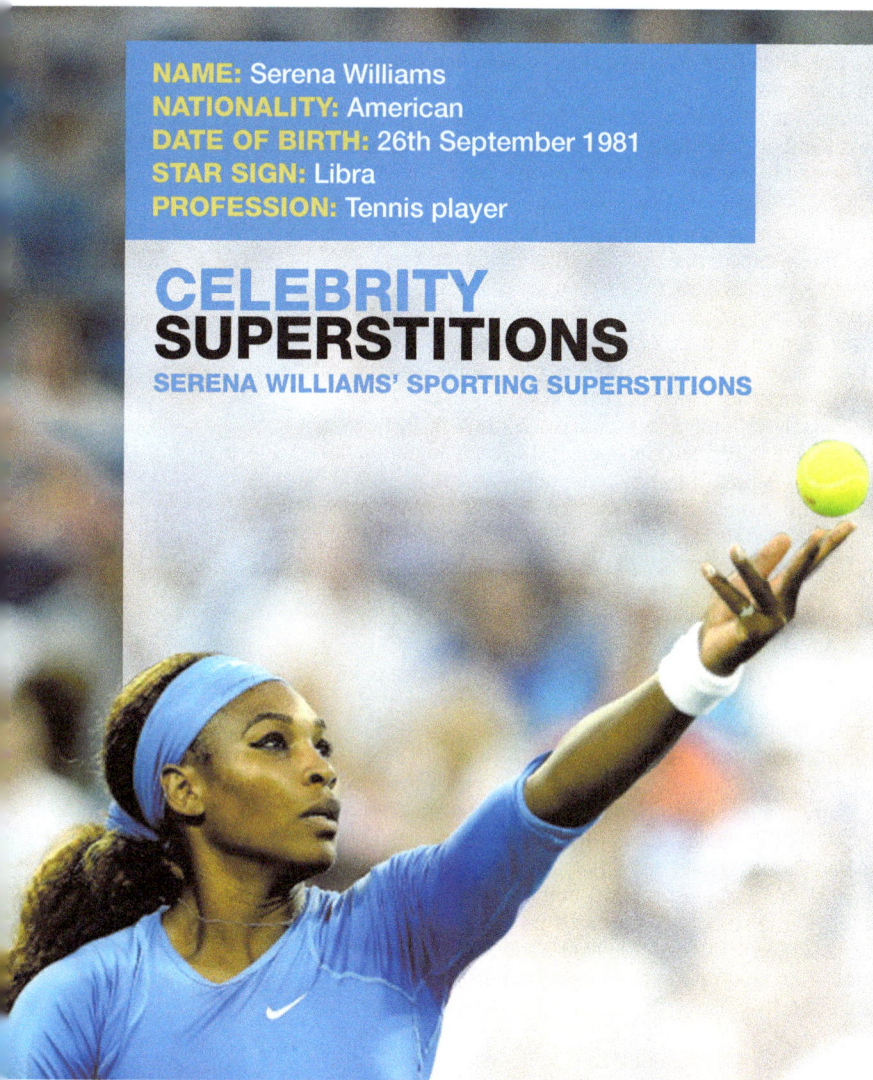

NAME: Serena Williams
NATIONALITY: American
DATE OF BIRTH: 26th September 1981
STAR SIGN: Libra
PROFESSION: Tennis player

CELEBRITY SUPERSTITIONS
SERENA WILLIAMS' SPORTING SUPERSTITIONS

1 ....
Serena is a famous American tennis player who has won many titles including Wimbledon, the French Open and the US Open. She has also been Olympic Singles and Doubles Champion. Serena is famous for being very competitive.

2 ....
Serena believes following special routines is the secret of her success. So she always:
- brings her shower sandals to the court.
- ties her shoelaces in a special way.
- bounces the ball five times before her first serve and two before the second.
- wears the same pair of socks for a whole tournament.

3 ....
Serena is always going to repeat this procedure to guarantee victory. She believes that she has lost matches because she has not followed those routines correctly.

4 ....
It is difficult to know how much this belief affects her performance on court – maybe there is some truth to this. After all, she is the most successful female tennis player of all time. For all the tennis players reading this, now you know what to do to improve your game. How many times you choose to bounce the ball is up to you!

Look

1 Read the text. Then cover the text and try to remember four things that Serena does to win the match. Compare your ideas with a partner.

2 Match the headings with the paragraphs.
   a   Why she follows the superstition
   b   Conclusion
   c   Background information
   d   What the superstition is

Prepare

3 Work in groups of three or four. Choose a famous celebrity. Use the Internet, books or magazines to find information about him/her. Find out about …
   - his/her career.
   - what he/she has won.
   - any superstitions he/she has.

Present

4 Display the magazine article on the wall in your classroom. Ask your classmates to read it. Have a class vote to choose the strangest celebrity superstition.

Thanks and acknowledgements

The authors and publishers would like to thank all the teachers and consultants who have contributed to the development of this course, in particular:

Argentina: Fernando Armesto; Natalia Bitar; Verónica Borrás; Leonor Corradi ; Paz Moltrasio; Diana Ogando; Brazil: Dalmo Carvalho; Roberto Costa; Sônia M. B. Leites; Gloria Paz; Litany Pires Ribeiro; Christina Riego; Renata Condi de Souza; Elizabeth White; Chile: Magdalena Aldunate; M. Cristina Darraidou Diaz; Valentina Donoso; Ana María Páez Jofrré; Ricardo Contreras Marambio; Claudia Ottone; Maria Elena Ramirez; Jacqueline Rondon; Alicia Paez Ubilla; Colombia: Luz Amparo Bautista; Sonia Ruiz Hernández; Sandra Jara; Fabian Jimenez; Bibiana Andrea Piñeros Merizalde; Lucero Amparo Bernal Nieto; Olga Olarte; Bibiana Piñeros; Emelis Rambut; Sonia Ruíz; Poland: Anna Bylicka; Russia: Natalya Melchenkova; Irina Polyakova; Svetlana Suchkova; Irina Vayserberg; Turkey: Ali Bilgin; Angela Çakır; Shirley Nuttal; Cinla Sezgin; Mujgan Yesiloglu

The publishers are grateful to the following for permission to reproduce copyright photographs and material:
Cover: Alamy/©Martin Strimska; Back cover: Shutterstock Images/fluke samed; p. 6 (BR): Shutterstock Images/Prometheus72; p. 6 (TL): Alamy/©Stockbroker; p. 7 (TL): Shutterstock Images/Jacek Chabraszewski; p. 7 (TC): Shutterstock Images/scyther5; p. 7 (BC): Shutterstock Images/Ervin Monn; p. 8 (B/G): Getty Images/Stone; p. 9 (a): Shutterstock Images/Tom Wang; p. 9 (b): Shutterstock Images/fluke samed; p. 9 (c): Alamy/©blickwinkel; p. 9 (d): Alamy/©David R. Frazier Photolibrary Inc.; p. 9 (e): Shutterstock Images/egd; p. 9 (f): Shutterstock Images/Richard Whitcombe; p. 9 (g): Shutterstock Images/Igumnova Irina; p. 9 (h): Shutterstock Images/James BO Insogna; p. 10 (B): Alamy/©RIA Novosti; p. 10 (BC): Alamy/©RIA Novosti; p. 11 (TR): Alamy/©Kumar Sriskandan; p. 12-13 (B/G): Alamy/©Paul Mayall Australia; p. 14 (B/G T): Alamy/©Plinthpics; p. 14 (BR): Alamy/©Ben Pipe; p. 14 (C): Alamy/©Images of Africa Photobank; p. 14 (TR): Alamy/©Trish Ainslie; p. 14-15 (B/G): Alamy/©Chris Howarth/South Atlantic; p. 16 (TR): Alamy/©Ellen Isaacs; p. 16 (BR): Alamy/© VIEW Pictures Ltd/; p. 17 (TR): Alamy/©Tim Graham; p. 17 (BR): Shutterstock Images/Burro; p. 18 (B/G): Corbis/2/Arctic-Images/Ocean; p. 19 (a): Alamy/©Tetra Images; p. 19 (b): Alamy/©Kuttig - People; p. 19 (c): Alamy/©Justin Kase zsixz; p. 19 (d): Shutterstock Images/Masson; p. 19 (e): Shutterstock Images/kuznetcov_konstantin; p. 19 (f): Superstock/age footstock; p. 19 (g): Getty Images/Image Source; p. 19 (h): REX/Phanie/Garo; p. 20 (T): Getty Images/Susanne Walstrom/Johner Images; p. 22 (TR): Shutterstock Images/bullet74; p. 22 (BR): Alamy/©The Art Archive; p. 23 (BC): Shutterstock Images/Helder Almeida; p. 24 (T): Alamy/©Paul Doyle; p. 24 (CR): Alamy/©ZUMA Press Inc.; p. 25 (B/G): Alamy/©Ulrich Doering; p. 25 (BL): Alamy/©LondonPhotos - Homer Sykes; p. 26 (BL): Alamy/©Kumar Sriskandan; p. 26 (CR): Alamy/©Blend Images; p. 27 (TL): Getty Images/Cavan Images/Taxi; p. 27 (TC): Getty Images/Steve Mason/Photodisc; p. 27 (CL): Shutterstock Images/Anna Jurkovska; p. 30 (B/G): Alamy/©Nikreates; p. 31 (a): Alamy/©Ian Francis; p. 31 (b): Alamy/©Arco Images GmbH; p. 31 (c): Alamy/©JOHN KELLERMAN; p. 31 (d): Alamy/©Andrew Aitchison; p. 31 (e): Corbis/ Sylvain Sonnet; p. 31 (f): Alamy/©eddie linssen; p. 31 (g): Alamy/©Ferenc Szelepcsenyi; p. 31 (h): Getty Images/Getty Images Sport/Andy Lyons; p. 31 (i): Alamy/©Michele and Tom Grimm; p. 31 (j): Alamy/©Artepics; p. 32 (BL): Alamy/©LOOK Die Bildagentur der Fotografen GmbH; p. 33 (TR): Corbis/ Bernd Kammerer/dpa; p. 33 (BL): Getty Images/Maartje Van Caspel; p. 34 (1): Shutterstock Images/Andrey_Popov; p. 34 (2): Shutterstock Images/mphot; p. 34 (3): Shutterstock Images/Vereshchagin Dmitry; p. 34 (4): Shutterstock Images/Redkaya; p. 34 (5): Shutterstock Images/Furtseff; p. 34 (6): Shutterstock Images/vvoe; p. 34 (7): Shutterstock Images/grigiomedio; p. 34 (8): Shutterstock Images/J. Helgason; p. 34 (9): Shutterstock Images/Dario Sabljak; p. 34 (10): Shutterstock Images/Chromakey; p. 34 (11): Shutterstock Images/Visun Khankasem; p. 34 (12): Shutterstock Images/Mike Braune; p. 34 (13): Shutterstock Images/Jouke van Keulen; p. 34 (14): Alamy/©Aki; p. 34 (TR): Alamy/©i stage; p. 36 (a): Alamy/©Richard Ellis; p. 36 (b): Alamy/©Stephen Chung; p. 36 (c): Alamy/©Universal Images Group Limited; p. 37 (C): REX/KeystoneUSA-ZUMA; p. 37 (CR): Getty Images/r e y . t o r r e s/Moment Open; p. 37 (BR): Alamy/©ZUMA Press, Inc.; p. 38 (CL): Corbis/Dirk Lindner; p. 39 (TC): Alamy/©Gari Wyn Williams; p. 39 (TL): Alamy/©david pearson; p. 40 (B/G): Alamy/©Michael Jones/Alaska Stock; p. 41 (a): ©CUP/Mark Bassett; p. 41 (b): Alamy/©AugustSnow; p. 41 (c): Alamy/©Dmitry Burlakov; p. 41 (d): Getty Images/Ken Chernus/Taxi; p. 41 (e): Shutterstock Images/PhotoSky; p. 41 (f): Alamy/©ZUMA Press, Inc.; p. 41 (g): Shutterstock Images/wavebreakmedia; p. 41 (h): Shutterstock Images/Johnny Adolphson; p. 41 (i): Shutterstock Images/ Stephen B. Goodwin; p. 42 (BC): Alamy/©ianmurray; p. 42 (BR): Alamy/©Mar Photographics; p. 44 (TL): Alamy/©Alibi Productions; p. 45 (CR): Alamy/©Purepix; p. 46 (TR): Shutterstock Images/Lev Kropotov; p. 46 (TC): Alamy/©Howard Davies; p. 46 (B/G): Shutterstock Images/Tooykrub; p. 47 (BR): Alamy/©Blaine Harrington III; p. 47 (TR): Alamy/©Allstar Picture Library; p. 47 (TC): Agefotostock/Stuart Blac; p. 48 (TL): Alamy/©Hemis; p. 48 (CR): Shutterstock Images/Strahil Dimitrov; p. 48 (BR): Alamy/©PhotoAlto; p. 49 (TR): Alamy/©Jochen Tack; p. 49 (TL): Alamy/©Wim Wiskerke; p. 50 (BR): Shutterstock Images/Gigi Peis; p. 51 (CR): Shutterstock Images/S.Borisov; p. 52 (B/G): Getty Images/Riou; p. 53 (a): Alamy/©Catchlight Visual Services; p. 53 (b): Alamy/©Buzzshotz; p. 53 (c): Alamy/©Anatolii Babii; p. 53 (d): Alamy/©IanDagnall Computing; p. 53 (e): Alamy/©NetPhotos; p. 53 (f): Alamy/©pumkinpie; p. 54-55 (b): Alamy/©Eric Audras; p. 56 (a): Shutterstock Images/Goran Djukanovic; p. 56 (b): Alamy/©John Powell/ Bubbles Photolibrary; p. 56 (c): Shutterstock Images/Tomasz Trojanowski; p. 56 (d): Alamy/©Blend Images; p. 57 (C): Alamy/©eye35.pix; p. 58 (T): Alamy/©Iain Masterton; p. 58 (CL): Alamy/©AKP Photos; p. 59 (BL): Alamy/©Top Photo/Asia Photo Connection/Henry Westheim Photography; p. 59 (BR): Shutterstock Images/Elena Elisseeva; p. 59 (TL): Alamy/©Bazza; p. 59 (BC): Alamy/©Liquid Light; p. 60 (TL): Alamy/©Valerie Garner; p. 60 (BL): Shutterstock Images/Deborah Kolb; p. 61 (TL): Shutterstock Images/Alexey Boldin; p. 62 (B/G): Getty Images/Jay P. Morgan; p. 63 (B/G): Shutterstock Images/Salajean; p. 63 (a): Alamy/©Robin Beckham/BEEPstock; p. 63 (b): Shutterstock Images/Jayakumar; p. 63 (c): Shutterstock Images/Dmitrijs Bindemanis; p. 63 (d): Shutterstock Images/Matteo photos; p. 63 (e): Shutterstock Images/Lisa F. Young; p. 63 (f): Shutterstock Images/Jag_cz; p. 64 (BC): Shutterstock Images/Sarah2; p. 64 (TC): Alamy/©Radius Images; p. 64 (C): Shutterstock Images/juniart; p. 64 (B): Alamy/©Image Source; p. 65 (BL): /Shutterstock Images/Sergei A. Aleshi; p. 66 (L): Alamy/©Gunter Marx; p. 66 (C): Getty Images/Petri Artturi Asikainen/Folio Images; p. 66 (R): Superstock/Greer & Associates, Inc.; p. 67 (TL): Alamy/©Ruby; p. 68 (TR): Alamy/©Peter Horree; p. 68 (BL): Alamy/©Tuul/Robert Harding World Imagery; p. 68 (B/G): Alamy/©Dbimages; p. 69 (BL): Alamy/©Adrian Turner; p. 69 (CR): Alamy/©David Gee; p. 69 (CL): Shutterstock Images/Sergio Foto; p. 69 (TR): Alamy/©Photodreams1; p. 69 (TL): Alamy/©Felipe Rodriguez; p. 69 (BR): Shutterstock Images/Olga Selyutina; p. 69 (CT):

Shutterstock Images/ Erni; p. 70 (CL): Alamy/©James Nesterwitz; p. 70 (CR): Getty Images/Echo/ultura; p. 70 (BR): Superstock/Marka; p. 71 (T): Getty Images/Elisabeth Schmitt/Moment Select; p. 72 (CR): Alamy/©Blue Jean Images; p. 73(TR): Shutterstock Images/cvrestan; p. 74 (B/G): Alamy/©Jennifer Podis/The Palm Beach Post/Zuma press; p. 75 (a): Alamy/©RubberBall; p. 75 (b): Alamy/©Westend61 GmbH; p. 75 (c): Corbis/©David Lefranc; p. 75 (d): Alamy/©imageBROKER; p. 75 (e): Shutterstock Images/BKMCphotography; p. 75 (f): Superstock/Image Source; p. 75 (g): Alamy/©Beyond Fotomedia GmbH; p. 75 (i): Getty Images/Silvia Otte/Taxi; p. 75 (f): Superstock/Image Source; p. 75 (h): Alamy/©Wavebreakmedia Ltd UC1; p. 76-77 (B): Alamy/©Riedmiller; p. 79 (CR): Alamy/©kt spencer march; p. 80 (TR): Getty Images/Inti St Clair/Digital Vision; p. 80 (TL): Alamy/©Ian Shaw; p. 80 (CR): Alamy/©Gregg Vignal; p. 81 (B/G): Shutterstock Images/oksana.perkins; p. 82 (TR): Alamy/©Image Source; p. 82 (CR): Alamy/©Tony Cordoza; p. 82 (BR): Alamy/©Marjorie Kamys Cotera/Bob Daemmrich Photography; p. 84 (B/G): Shutterstock Images/majeczka; p. 85 (a): Alamy/©imageBROKER; p. 85 (b): Alamy/©Steffen Hauser/botanikfoto; p. 85 (c): Q2A Media; p. 85 (d): Shutterstock Images/Sakarin Sawasdinaka; p. 85 (e): Q2A Media; p. 85 (f): Alamy/©Tom Merton/OJO Images Ltd; p. 85 (g): Q2A Media; p. 85 (h): Shutterstock Images/Kati Molin; p. 85 (i): Shutterstock Images/graphyx; p. 85 (j): Alamy/©Milena Boniek; p. 86 (CL): Alamy/©ZUMA Press; p. 86 (BL): Alamy/©Jay Goebel; p. 86-87 (B): Rex Features/Paul Cooper; p. 87 (TR): Corbis/Kirsten Neumann/Reuters; p. 88 (TL): Alamy/©Bubbles Photolibrary; p. 89 (B): Shutterstock Images/ Subbotina Anna; p. 90 (TL): Alamy/©US Labor Department; p. 90 (BL): Alamy/©Craig Ruttle; p. 90 (T): Getty Images/ Willoughby Owen; p. 91(CR): Shutterstock Images/Tchara; p. 91 (BR): Shutterstock Images/Daniel Schweinert; p. 91 (TR): Alamy/©Clynt Garnham Renewable Energy; p. 92 (BL): Superstock/imageBROKER; p. 92 (CR): Getty Images/Karl Lehmann/Lonely Planet Images; p. 92 (BR): Shutterstock Images/spwidoff; p. 93 (T): Alamy/©Todd Bannor; p. 93 (TR): Alamy/©Dave Porter; p. 95 (TR): Getty Images/Chris Schmidt; p. 107 (TR): Alamy/©Alaska Stock; p. 108 (TL): REX/Garo/ Phanie; p. 108 (TR): Shutterstock Images/Masson; p. 108 (BR): Alamy/©Ted Foxx; p. 108 (BL): Alamy/©Blend Images; p. 109 (TR): Alamy/©Arco Images GmbH; p. 109 (BL): Alamy/©eddie linssen; p. 109 (TL): Alamy/©Alex Segre; p. 109 (BR): Shutterstock Images/koi88; p. 110 (TC): Getty Images/Ken Chernus; p. 110 (TR): Shutterstock Images/Stephen B. Goodwin; p. 110 (C): Shutterstock Images/Johnny Adolphson; p. 110 (BR): Alamy/©Juice Images; p. 111 (TR): Getty Images/Silvia Otte/Taxi; p. 111 (TL): Alamy/©IS831/Image Source; p. 111 (BL): Alamy/©pumkinpie; p. 111 (BR): Alamy/©Anatolii Babii; p. 112 (TL): Shutterstock Images/Jag_cz; p. 112 (TR): Shutterstock Images/Matteo photos; p. 112 (BL): Shutterstock Images/Lisa F. Young; p. 112 (BR): Alamy/©Sigrid Olsson/PhotoAlto; p. 113 (TL): Alamy/©David L. Moore - Lifestyle; p. 113 (BL): Shutterstock Images/OLJ Studio; p. 113 (TR): Corbis/David Lefranc; p. 113 (BR): Shutterstock Images/BKMCphotography; p. 114 (TR): Alamy/©John Elk III; p. 114 (TL): Shutterstock Images/Dja65; p. 115 (T): Getty Images/peplow/iStock/360; p. 117 (TR): Bridgeman Art Library / Musee Marmottan, Paris, France / Giraudon; p. 117(BL): Alamy/©Painting; p. 119 (TL): Alamy/©emanja Radovanovic; p. 120 (L1): Getty Images/Songquan Deng/iStock/360; p. 120 (L2): Getty Images/Matthew Dixon/iStock/360; p. 120 (R1): Alamy/©Geoff Marshall; p. 120 (R2): Shutterstock Images/Art Konovalov; p. 121 (TR): Getty Images/Christopher Futcher/iStock/360; p. 121 (CR): Shutterstock Images/febri ardi Antonius; p. 122 (C):Alamy/©Paul Lindsay; p. 122 (TC): Shutterstock Images/jaroslava V; p. 123 (TL): actionplus sports images; p. 123 (CL): Alamy/©Stephen Barnes/Sport; p. 124 (C): Getty Images/Matthew Stockman/Getty Images Sport; p. 125 (TL): Corbis/Lea Suzuki/San Francisco Chronicle; p. 125 (TR): Superstock/Science and Society/Science and Society; p. 125 (BR): Shutterstock Images/Serdiukov; p. 125 (CR): Shutterstock Images/ Matusciac Alexandru; p. 125 (CL): Shutterstock Images/Viktor Prymachenko; p. 125 (BL): Shutterstock Images/Africa Studio.

The publishers are grateful to the following illustrators:
David Belmonte (Beehive Illustration): p. 116; Anni Betts p. 4, 38; Nigel Dobbyn (Beehive Illustration): p. 78; Mark Duffin p. 12, 116; Guy Pearce p. 35; Sean Tiffany p. 5; Q2A Media Services, Inc. p. 5, 14, 15, 24, 36, 37, 46, 47, 58, 68, 80, 90, 91, 118; Tony Wilkins p. 115, 118.

All video stills by kind permission of:
Discovery Communications, LLC 2015: p. 8(1, 2, 4), 11, 14, 18 (1, 2, 4), 21, 24, 30 (1, 2, 4), 33, 36, 40 (1, 2, 4), 43, 46, 52 (1, 2, 4), 55, 58, 62 (1, 2, 4), 65, 68, 74 (1, 2, 4), 77, 80, 84 (1, 2, 4), 87, 90, 115, 116, 117, 118, 119, 120, 121, 122.

Cambridge University Press: 7, 8 (3), 16, 18 (3), 26, 30 (3), 38, 40 (3), 48, 52 (3), 60, 62 (3), 70, 74 (3), 84 (3), 92.

Corpus
Development of this publication has made use of the Cambridge English Corpus (CEC). The CEC is a computer database of contemporary spoken and written English, which currently stands at over one billion words. It includes British English, American English and other varieties of English. It also includes the Cambridge Learner Corpus, developed in collaboration with the University of Cambridge ESOL Examinations. Cambridge University Press has built up the CEC to provide evidence about language use that helps to produce better language teaching materials.

The publishers are grateful to the following contributors:
Blooberry: concept design
emc design limited: text design and layouts
QBS Learning: cover design and photo selection
Ian Harker and Dave Morritt at DSound: audio recordings
Integra: video production
Nick Bruckman and People's TV: voxpop video production
Hart McCleod: video voiceovers
Anna Whitcher: video management
BraveArts, S.L: additional audio recordings
Getty Images: music
Vicki Anderson: Speaking and Writing pages
Debbie Owen and Alice Martin: Starter Unit
Jose Luis Jiménez Maroto and Alice Martin: CLIL pages
Mick Green: Grammar Reference pages
Emma Szlachta: Editor & Vocabulary Bank
Debbie Owen and Alice Martin: Project pages
Diane Nicholls: Corpus research & Get it Right features

This page is intentionally left blank

Eyes Open 3 Combo A

WORKBOOK with Digital Pack

Vicki Anderson with Eoin Higgins

CAMBRIDGE UNIVERSITY PRESS

Discovery EDUCATION

Contents

	Starter Unit	page 3
1	**Extreme living**	page 7
2	**A balancing act**	page 17
3	**Art all around us**	page 27
4	**Adventure**	page 37
	Speaking extra	page 87
	Language focus extra	page 95

Starter Unit

Meeting people

1 ★ Put the sentences in the correct order to make a conversation.

___ **Karen and Jackie:** See you later!
___ **Jackie:** Hi Pete. Nice to meet you.
___ **Pete:** Hello. I'm Pete.
_1_ **Karen:** This is my friend. Her name's Jackie.
___ **Pete:** You too. Well, I have to go.
___ **Pete:** Yes, bye!
___ **Karen:** Hi. My name's Karen. What's your name?

Routines

2 ★ Complete the daily activities. Use the words in the box. Then number the activities in the order you do them every day.

go (x2)   do   ~~wake~~   get   have (x3)

___ _____ lunch
___ _____ to bed
___ _____ up
___ _____ breakfast
_1_ _wake_ up
___ _____ to school
___ _____ homework
___ _____ dinner

Free-time activities

3 ★★ Write the activities under the pictures. Use *do*, *go*, *play*, *read*, *sing*, or *watch*.

1. _play basketball_
2. _____
3. _____
4. _____
5. _____
6. _____
7. _____
8. _____

Starter Unit   3

Wh- questions

4 ⭐ **Complete the questions with the words in the box.**

> What   Where   When   How
> How old   Who   Whose

1. **A:** ___How old___ were you when you started playing tennis?
   B: I was 5 years old.
2. **A:** _____ did you go after school yesterday?
   B: I went to the swimming pool.
3. **A:** _____ is that girl over there?
   B: That's Giulia. She's Italian.
4. **A:** _____ are you doing?
   B: I'm sending a message to Oliver.
5. **A:** _____ phone number is this?
   B: It's Noah's. I have to call him later.
6. **A:** _____ did you go to Colombia?
   B: Last summer. It was great.
7. **A:** _____ do you switch on this tablet?
   B: It's easy. Press here.

Adjectives

5 ⭐ **Use the clues to complete the crossword.**

Across
4 makes you angry
7 strange
9 fantastic
10 makes you laugh

Down
1 makes you want to run away
2 someone that will help you
3 someone that doesn't like you
5 opposite of interesting
6 always smiling and positive
8 someone who cannot wait

Comparative and superlative adjectives

6 ⭐ **Circle the correct options.**
1. This film is much **more** / **most** frightening than that one.
2. What's the **easiest** / **easier** subject at school?
3. Many people think Real Madrid are **better** / **best** than all other football teams.
4. Playing a sport is much **more** / **most** exciting than watching one!
5. You can move **more fast** / **faster** in a city by motorbike than by car.
6. Dubai has got the **taller** / **tallest** building in the world.

Adverbs

7 ⭐ **Complete the sentences with the adverb form of the adjectives in brackets.**
1. I learned the song ___easily___ (easy) because I had a good teacher.
2. Jack draws very _____ (good). He's a very good artist.
3. That app is difficult to use. Read the instructions _____ (careful).
4. They walked _____ (slow) on the beach in the evening sun.
5. My dad plays basketball _____ (bad). He can't get the ball into the basket!
6. I chatted _____ (happy) for an hour with my friend Lola last night.
7. We should talk _____ (quiet) because my little brother's asleep.
8. Grace did her homework _____ (quick) because she wanted to watch TV.

4   Starter Unit

Comparative and superlative adverbs

8 ★★ Write sentences with the comparative or superlative forms of the adverbs.

1 Harry / learned / swim / easily / me
   Harry learned to swim more easily than me.
2 The man / ran / quickly / the police
   _____
3 They / played / the sad songs / quietly
   _____
4 He / spoke / slowly / than / the first time
   _____
5 My dad / drives / carefully / of all the family
   _____
6 Lydia / writes / good / me
   _____

Past simple

9 ★ Circle the correct words in the table.

1	In the past simple we add *-ed* or *-d* to the infinitive in **regular / irregular** verbs.
2	To form negatives, we put *didn't* + **infinitive / past form**.
3	To form questions, we put *Did* + subject + **infinitive / past form**.
4	We form negatives and questions of irregular verbs in **the same / a different** way.

10 ★★ Complete the text. Use the past simple form of the verbs in brackets.

Last year I ¹ *had* (have) a terrible experience when a shark ² _____ (attack) me. That day I ³ _____ (not see) the red danger flag at the beach, so I ⁴ _____ (decide) to go surfing. Suddenly I ⁵ _____ (hear) someone shouting, and the next minute I ⁶ _____ (see) the shark a few metres away from me. I ⁷ _____ (jump) off my surfboard, the shark ⁸ _____ (open) its mouth, and I ⁹ _____ (hit) it hard on the nose. The surfboard ¹⁰ _____ (break) in half. I don't know why, but the shark ¹¹ _____ (not attack) me again. It ¹² _____ (swim) away very fast. How lucky!

11 ★★ Write questions for a local politician. Use the prompts and the past simple.

1 What problems / the town / have?
   What problems did the town have?
2 So / you / build flood defences?
   _____
3 What / you / do?
   _____
4 How much / it / cost?
   _____
5 Where / you / get the money?
   _____
6 Why / people / start to call you a green town?
   _____

12 ★★ Complete the politician's answers. Use the verbs in the box in the past simple. Then match the answers (a–f) with the questions in Exercise 11.

~~reach~~	decide	give	have	move
not think	be	not pay		

a The total ¹ *reached* more than $6 million.
   Question: *4*
b Because we ² _____ to put solar panels on all the new buildings. We ³ _____ the first green town in the USA!
   Question: ___
c We ⁴ _____ terrible floods every two or three years because the town was by the river.
   Question: ___
d No, the experts ⁵ _____ that normal protection could stop the floods.
   Question: ___
e The town ⁶ _____ all the money. The government ⁷ _____ us $4 million.
   Question: ___
f The people of the town ⁸ _____ all the houses and shops up the hill!
   Question: ___

13 ★★ It is 8 o'clock in the evening. Look at the table and write sentences in the past simple about Dylan with *ago*.

8.00 am	12.00 pm	1.00 pm	5.00 pm	7.00 pm	7.55 pm
got up	had a Maths test	have lunch	go to the park	arrive home from judo class	wash his hands

1 *He got up twelve hours ago.*
2 _____
3 _____
4 _____
5 _____
6 _____

14 ★★ Answer the questions. Use *ago*.
1 When did you start school today?
Three hours ago.
2 When did you last go on holiday?
_____
3 When did you start to learn English?
_____
4 When did you have breakfast today?
_____
5 When did you last go to the park with your friends?
_____

Explaining a problem

15 ★★ Match the sentences with the correct place in the conversation.

A: William, what's the matter?
B: ¹ _b_
A: Oh no! Your Maths homework?
B: ² ___
A: OK, don't panic! Where did you put it when you finished it?
B: ³ ___
A: But it's not in your bag. Is it in your Maths book?
B: ⁴ ___
A: Why not?
B: ⁵ ___
A: Well, where could it be, then?
B: ⁶ ___
A: I hope so!

a Let me think. In the classroom? It's probably in there.
b I lost my homework.
c I'm not sure. I think I put it in my bag.
d No way!
e Yes. It took me over an hour. I don't know what to do.
f Well, for one thing. Why would I put it in my Maths book?

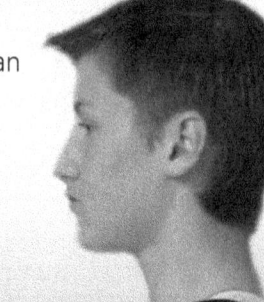

1 Extreme living

Vocabulary
Extreme weather

1 ★ **Complete the crossword. Use the pictures.**

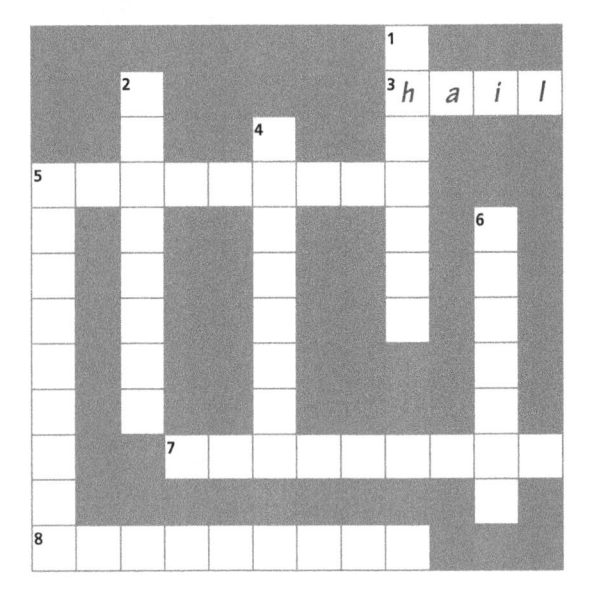

3 across: h a i l

Across

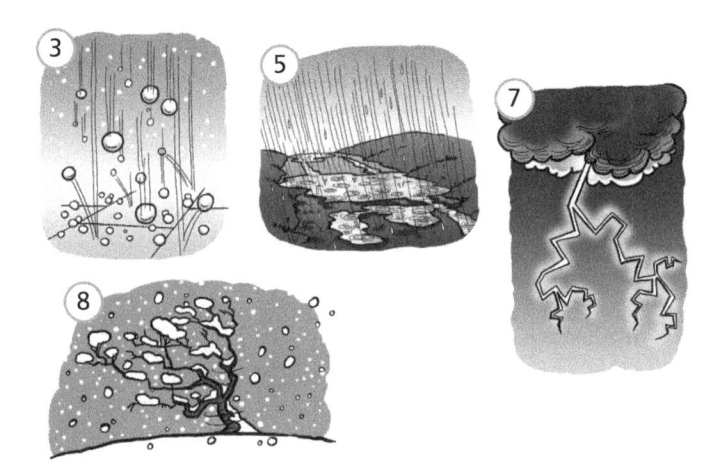

Down

2 ★ **Circle the odd one out.**
1 boiling   (heavy rain)   freezing
2 heatwave   boiling   high winds
3 heavy rain   thunder and lightning   freezing
4 hail   snowstorm   boiling
5 freezing   heatwave   snowstorm

3 ★★ **Complete the sentences with the correct form of the extreme weather words from Exercise 1.**
1 Germany has a lot of ___hail___ storms. Sometimes the stones are like tennis balls. They're enormous!
2 Moscow is the city with the most _____. It has 1,000 vehicles to remove snow!
3 In Helsinki there are 169 days below 0 °C. That's similar to Alaska! It's _____.
4 In the summer months there are _____ in many cities, which can kill people!
5 Écija near Córdoba is the hottest place in Europe. It's _____ there in August!
6 Amsterdam, Paris and Rome airports are having problems with _____ of over 100 km per hour.

4 ★★ **Complete the texts about the weather. Use the words in the box.**

rain ~~snowstorms~~ hail thunder
freezing lightning winds

Many European countries are in chaos this morning because of heavy ¹ _snowstorms_ , high ² _____ and ³ _____ temperatures. In Poland the temperature is –26 °C.

NEWS

Two hours ago
There's a spectacular storm here! The heavy ⁴ _____ means we can't go out. We can see ⁵ _____ over the sea, and hear the ⁶ _____ . It's very loud. It's cold too and sometimes there's ⁷ _____ . It's really big – I hope it doesn't break anything! What's the weather like where you are?

5 ★★★ **What's the weather like in spring, summer, autumn and winter in your country? Write sentences about the things in Exercise 1.**

We don't have snowstorms here very often, but it's usually boiling in the summer.

Unit 1   7

Language focus 1

Present simple vs. present continuous

1 ★ Choose the correct options.
1. When it's freezing, we **don't go** / **aren't going** out.
2. There's a snowstorm right now so we **stay** / **'re staying** at home.
3. I always **play** / **am playing** basketball on Saturdays.
4. The temperature **falls** / **is falling** each year in winter so there's a lot of snow.
5. I **learn** / **'m learning** German at the moment because I want to go to Germany in December.
6. It's 8 o'clock in the morning and I **have** / **'m having** breakfast.

2 ★ Complete the sentences with the correct form of the present simple or present continuous. Use the verbs in the box.

```
not spend   come   look   come
go   snow   not go
```

1. It's November and winter ___is coming___ in Canada.
2. It's very cold and silent today. _____ it _____ outside?
3. The polar bear _____ for a place to hibernate in winter.
4. We _____ much time at the beach in the autumn. It's very cold.
5. _____ you _____ to visit us this year?
6. I _____ skating today because there's no ice, but I usually _____ on Sundays.

3 ★★ Complete the mini-conversations. Use the present simple or the present continuous form of the verbs in brackets.
1. **A:** What ___is Laura doing___ (Laura do) at the moment?
   B: She _____ (be) on holiday with her parents, I think.
2. **A:** What _____ usually _____ (you do) at the weekends?
   B: Not much, so I _____ (enjoy) this camping trip. It's great!
3. **A:** _____ (you make) a cake for the party?
   B: Yes, but we _____ (not know) what to do next! _____ (we do) it right?

4 ★★ Complete the interview with a park ranger. Use the present simple or the present continuous form of the verbs in brackets.

Interviewer: Today I [1] ___'m talking___ (talk) to Safri, who's a ranger at the Royal Belum State Park, Malaysia. Safri, what [2] _____ a park ranger _____ (do)?
Safri: Well, we [3] _____ (protect) wild animals from hunters, and we [4] _____ (look) after the park. I [5] _____ (work) here this summer because the permanent rangers [6] _____ (not have) much free time to spend with visitors. All this week I [7] _____ (tell) visitors about our work here and I [8] _____ (show) them the animals. It [9] _____ (be) a great job!

5 ★★★ Complete the email with the correct form of the present simple or present continuous. Use the verbs in the box.

```
have (x2)   play   sit   rain   do (x2)
not go   go   run
```

✉ **New Message**   Send   Cancel

Hi Kim,
Well, here I am in Scotland! I [1] ___'m sitting___ in my room. It [2] _____ again so people [3] _____ down the streets. There's another girl in my house called Carmen. She [4] _____ a shower right now. We [5] _____ out this afternoon. We usually [6] _____ two English classes in the morning and in the afternoon we [7] _____ our homework and [8] _____ sports. On Wednesdays, we often go swimming but I [9] _____ today because Carmen wants to go to the cinema. [10] _____ you _____ anything interesting? Write and tell me!
Eva

6 ★★★ Choose a place and invent a special weekend. Imagine you are there. Write at least five sentences about it.

I'm in Rome at the moment with .... We're sitting in ...

8   Unit 1

Listening and vocabulary

Survival essentials

1 ★ **Add vowels to the words to make travel essentials.**

TRCH   CMR   ~~CNTCT LNSS~~   PNKNF
SLPNG BG   CMPSS   MP   WTR BTTL
FRST D KT   SNGLSSS   SN CRM   GLSSS

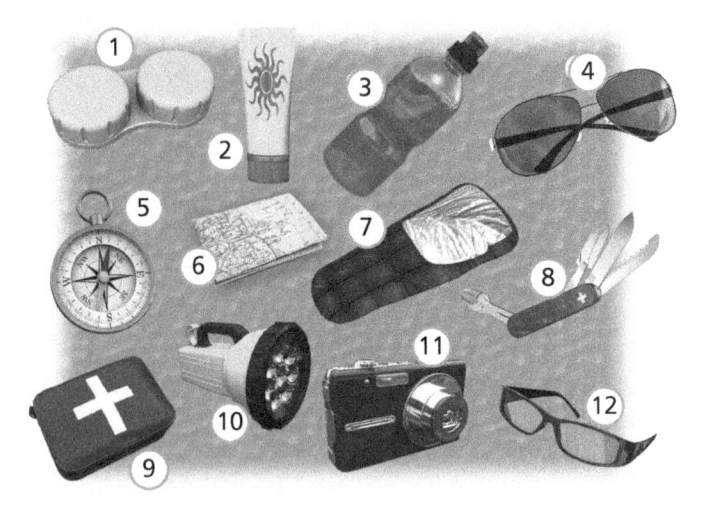

1	_contact lenses_	7	_____
2	_____	8	_____
3	_____	9	_____
4	_____	10	_____
5	_____	11	_____
6	_____	12	_____

2 ★★ **Complete the text with words for travel essentials from Exercise 1.**

We had a scary experience in the mountains last weekend. There was a landslide! And now I know why Dad always tells me to pack my bag carefully before we go walking. The ¹ _first aid kit_ was essential because a rock hit me. I didn't have a lot of water in my ² _____ but I cleaned the cut in the river. We couldn't continue our route because of the landslide, and it was very late so we stayed the night in the forest. It was very dark but we had the ³ _____ , and my ⁴ _____ was very warm. Another problem was that I didn't have the case for my ⁵ _____ , but I can't sleep in them so I put them in a plastic cup. For breakfast the next morning we only had some old bread and cheese. The bread was hard but I had my ⁶ _____ to cut it with. After that we used the ⁷ _____ and ⁸ _____ to find another way home and we finally arrived home after five hours, really tired!!

Listening

3 ★ 🔊 01 **Listen to the story of Laurie, a Canadian teenager, on a radio programme called 'Lucky escapes'. What did she escape from and how?**

4 ★★ 🔊 01 **Listen again and answer the questions.**
1. Where is Laurie from?
   She's from Canada.
2. When did the story happen?
   _____
3. Why was Laurie in the forest?
   _____
4. Why did they realise they were in danger?
   _____
5. What did they take with them?
   _____
6. Why did they start running?
   _____
7. How did they find the river?
   _____
8. How did they travel down the river?
   _____
9. Why was the torch useful?
   _____
10. How many hours were they in the river?
    _____

Unit 1 9

Language focus 2

Past simple vs. past continuous

1 ★ Circle the correct options.
1. They **cancelled** / were cancelling our flight because a volcano **erupted** / was erupting two days before in Iceland.
2. Where **did you go** / were you going when I **saw** / was seeing you in the street?
3. A police officer **stopped** / was stopping us from going into our house because there **was** / was being a big fire.
4. When the river water **rose** / was rising after the heavy rain, it **came** / was coming near the town centre.
5. While the rescue workers **looked** / were looking for people, they **found** / were finding a little boy.
6. The lights **came** / were coming on again while I **looked** / was looking for my torch.
7. I **cut** / was cutting my finger when I **used** / was using the penknife.
8. Ellie **fell** / was falling over while she **ran** / was running away from the fire.

2 ★★ Write sentences with the prompts.

1. When / I / watch TV / the lights / go out
   When I was watching TV, the lights went out.
2. When / we / see the landslide / we / drive home
   _____
3. She / ski / when / she / hear / the avalanche
   _____
4. The rescue helicopter / arrive / when / the family / phone for help
   _____
5. A fire fighter / give them / water / when / they / wait for an ambulance
   _____
6. I / drink / from my water bottle / when / I / see / a helicopter
   _____

3 ★★ Circle the correct options in the text.

In 2012 there was a serious earthquake in Guatemala. When it ¹**happened** / was happening, fire fighter Tina Watson ² watched / was watching TV at home in Los Angeles. But only two days later, she and Chester, her search and rescue dog, ³ flew / was flying into Guatemala to help. On the first day, they ⁴ found / were finding two survivors, but on the second day they ⁵ didn't find / weren't finding any. Then, on the third day, Tina and Chester ⁶ searched / were searching an apartment block, when they ⁷ located / were locating three teenage girls trapped in the ruins. They were very thirsty, so Chester ⁸ took / was taking them Tina's water bottle until more rescue workers ⁹ arrived / were arriving. Amazingly, when they finally ¹⁰ pulled / were pulling the girls out, they weren't injured.

4 ★★★ Write sentences that are true for you about five of the times in the box. Use the past simple or the past continuous.

25th December 2013   yesterday at 1 pm
last August   this time last Saturday
my last birthday   9 o'clock on Sunday morning

This time last Saturday I was watching a film with my friends.

Explore prepositional phrases

5 ★★ Complete the sentences with the prepositional phrases in the box.

on the planet   in both directions   on a ship
on the island   ~~on the Internet~~

1. You shouldn't believe everything you read *on the Internet* .
2. The Antarctic is one of the coldest places _____ .
3. It's only four kilometres from the coast but nobody lives _____ .
4. We looked left and right but there was nothing but houses _____ .
5. There are no flights so you have to travel _____ to the island.

10   Unit 1

Reading

1 ★ Read the text about Matt Suter. What unusual thing happened to him? How old was he?

Matt Suter, from Missouri, USA, is lucky to be *alive*. In 2006 he became one of the few people to experience the inside of a tornado and survive.

Matt was a high-school student at the time and was relaxing at home in his grandmother's *trailer* when he heard a noise like a jet plane, which got louder and louder. One minute he realised that the walls and the floor of the trailer were moving, and the next minute all the windows and doors exploded. It was a tornado.

A lamp hit Matt on the head, and he *lost consciousness*. At that moment the tornado *sucked* him out of the trailer and he disappeared. When he woke up, he was lying in a *field* of soft grass, a long way from the trailer. His head was *bleeding* where the lamp hit him and his feet were cut, but surprisingly, that was all. A neighbour found him, and they went to look for his grandmother. Luckily, she also survived, under the ruins of the trailer.

The tornado carried 19-year-old Matt nearly 400 metres from the trailer and then dropped him. Now he *holds* a strange world *record*: he is the person to travel the longest distance in a tornado and survive! For a while he was a celebrity. He appeared on television to talk about his experience, but he didn't have very much to say because, unfortunately, he can't remember anything about what happened after the lamp *knocked* him *out*!

2 ★★ Match the words in the box with the definitions. Use the words in **bold** in the text to help you.

field   alive   trailer   suck   bleed   ~~lose consciousness~~
hold a record   knock (someone) out

1 go into an unconscious state (like sleep) _lose consciousness_
2 the opposite of dead _____
3 a piece of farmland _____
4 a mobile home or caravan _____
5 lose blood in an accident _____
6 be the best person in the world at something _____
7 hit someone and make them unconscious _____
8 pull into your mouth _____

3 ★★ Read the text again. Put the events in order.
a Matt found his grandmother. ___
b The tornado lifted Matt and carried him away. ___
c He appeared on TV. ___
d Matt was relaxing in his grandmother's trailer. _1_
e Matt woke up in a field. ___
f A tornado hit the trailer. ___
g A lamp hit Matt on the head. ___

4 ★★ Read the text again. Are these sentences true (*T*) or false (*F*)? Correct the false sentences.
1 Matt Suter is from England. *F*
   Matt Suter is from the USA.
2 Matt was 19 when the tornado happened.
   _____
3 A plane hit the trailer where Matt was.
   _____
4 Matt landed on a road 400 metres from the trailer.
   _____
5 The lamp hit Matt after the tornado hit the trailer.
   _____
6 The police found Matt in a field.
   _____
7 His grandma didn't die in the tornado.
   _____
8 Matt told everyone how it felt to be in a tornado.
   _____

5 ★★★ Imagine Matt is giving a TV interview. Write at least five questions and answers.

Interviewer: How did it start?
Matt: Well … I was sitting in our trailer when I heard a loud noise.

Writing

An email to a friend

1 Read the email from Joe to his friend Ricky. What's the weather like on his holiday?

> Hi Ricky,
> Thanks ¹_for_ your ²_____ .
> It's ³_____ to ⁴_____ from you!
> We're having a fantastic holiday in Arizona! We're visiting national parks in a camper van. We cook all our meals in the van and we sleep in sleeping bags outdoors under the stars – with a torch of course. I love it! At the moment we're in the Petrified Forest National Park. There's a photo attached – isn't it amazing? There are lots of fossils from 225 million years ago! We love walking, but it's boiling during the day so we try to go early in the morning before the temperature rises. We always bring sun cream and water bottles.
> ⁵_____ are you doing at the ⁶_____ ?
> Are you enjoying your holidays?
> Write ⁷_____ soon,
> Best wishes,
> Joe

2 Complete the email from Joe to his friend Ricky. Use the words in the box. There are four extra words.

> moment ~~for~~ great what get
> soon email tell your back hear

Useful language — Opening and closing an email

3 Read Joe's email again. How does he open and close the email?
Opening: ¹_____ Ricky,
Closing: ²_____ , ³_____

4 Complete the phrases for opening and closing an email with the words you didn't use in Exercise 2.
1 Write back and ____tell____ me your news.
2 It was great to _____ your email.
3 Hope to hear from you _____ .
4 How are you and _____ family?

12 Unit 1

Writing

5 Put the words in order to make questions.
1. moment / are / What / doing / at / you / the?
   What are you doing at the moment?
2. good time / you / Are / having / a?
   _____
3. going / you / Where / holiday / on / are?
   _____
4. do / day / you / What / do / the / during?
   _____
5. you are / What's / where / the / like / weather?
   _____
6. a / send / Can / photo / you / me?
   _____

6 Complete the sentences with the correct prepositions of time.
1. We sleep in sleeping bags ____*at*____ night.
2. We start walking _____ it gets too hot.
3. We're on holiday in Canada _____ the moment.
4. What do you do _____ the day?
5. There are a lot of things to do _____ the morning.

> **WRITING TIP**
> Make it better! ✓✓✓
> Use negative questions to ask the reader to agree with you and to show surprise.

7 Use the words to make negative questions.
1. photo / amazing
   Isn't the photo amazing?
2. boiling / during the day?
   _____
3. you / be / on holiday / yet?
   _____
4. want / sleep under the stars?
   _____
5. my new sunglasses / cool?
   _____
6. the summer / great?
   _____

8 Read the email again. Number the things in the list in the order they appear.

transport	___	weather	___
accommodation	___	activities	___
place in now	*1*	interesting facts	___

PLAN

9 Imagine you are on holiday in an exciting place. Use the headings in Exercise 8 and your imagination. Write notes.

WRITE

10 Write an email to a friend about your holiday. Look at page 17 of the Student's Book to help you.

_____
_____
_____
_____
_____
_____
_____
_____
_____
_____
_____
_____
_____
_____

CHECK

11 Check your writing. Can you say YES to these questions?
- Is the information from Exercise 8 in your email?
- Have you got opening and closing phrases in your email?
- Are the prepositions of time correct?
- Do you use negative questions for surprise?
- Is the word order in the questions correct?
- Are the spelling and punctuation correct?

Do you need to write a second draft?

1 Review

Vocabulary
Extreme weather

1 Match the words with the correct definitions.

1. hail
2. boiling
3. thunder
4. freezing
5. lightning
6. heavy rain

a very hot
b very wet weather
c very cold
d small pieces of ice
e flashes of electricity in the sky
f a loud crashing noise in a storm

Total: 5

Survival essentials

2 Complete the sentences with the words in the box.

> camera   torch   ~~compass~~   sunglasses
> penknife   map   sun cream
> contact lenses   water bottle
> sleeping bag

1. We'll have to use the ___compass___ to find the right direction.
2. Look at the _____ and that will help you plan your journey.
3. Take a _____ so you can see in the dark.
4. I've got a _____ so we can take pictures.
5. You should use _____ to protect your skin.
6. Do you use _____ to help you see better, or glasses?
7. I always carry a _____ to cut my food.
8. Don't forget your _____ to protect your eyes from the sun.
9. We'll take a _____ so that we are warm at night.
10. Have you got a _____ to carry something to drink?

Total: 9

Language focus
Present simple vs. present continuous

3 Complete the mini-conversations with the present simple or present continuous form of the verbs in brackets.

1. A: Is she doing her homework? (do homework)
   B: Yes, ___she is___.
   A: _____? (always / do homework / in her bedroom)
   B: Yes, _____.

2. A: What _____? (do)
   B: He _____. (run a marathon)
   A: How often _____? (he / train)
   B: He _____. (train / every day)

3. A: _____? (read a book)
   B: No, _____.
   A: _____? (like reading)
   B: No, _____.

Total: 10

Past simple vs. past continuous

4 Complete the text. Use the past simple or the past continuous form of the verbs in brackets.

NARROW ESCAPE for mountain hikers

A group of hikers ¹___had___ a close escape when they ²_____ (hike) in the mountains last Friday. 'At around midnight, I ³_____ (look) at the stars when suddenly I ⁴_____ (see) a bright light in the sky. I ⁵_____ (not know) what to do! The others ⁶_____ (sleep) in their tents so I woke them up and we all ⁷_____ (run) to our car and ⁸_____ (drive) away as fast as possible,' said Rob, one of the hikers. 'Fortunately, we ⁹_____ (escape)!'

Total: 8

UNIT 1

Language builder

5 Complete the email with the missing words. Circle the correct options.

1. a have   b are having   c do have
2. a were sailing   b was sailing   c sailed
3. a see   b were seeing   c saw
4. a waked up   b were waking up   c woke up
5. a is   b did be   c was
6. a had   b have   c were having
7. a hardly ever erupts   b erupts hardly ever   c hardly erupts ever
8. a in the year   b in year   c a year
9. a take   b took   c 'm taking
10. a 'm wrote   b write   c wrote

Total: 9

Your MAIL + New   Reply | ▼ Delete

Dear Sue,

We ¹___ a wonderful time on our holiday in Oregon. Last weekend, we ²___ along the coast when we ³___ some whales. And yesterday morning, we ⁴___ to see a cloud of white smoke at the top of the mountain. It ⁵___ a volcanic eruption! They ⁶___ a really big eruption here a few years ago, but now the volcano ⁷___ – maybe once ⁸___ or less. I ⁹___ lots of photos of it! Don't forget I ¹⁰___ in my blog every day so you can read all my news there.

See you soon,
Julie

Vocabulary builder

6 Circle the correct options.

1. Are you ___ swimming now?
   a doing   b going   c playing
2. We can't go anywhere. There's a big ___ outside.
   a hail   b snowstorm   c rain
3. How many people live ___ the island?
   a in   b at   c on
4. We're laughing because this photo is very ___ .
   a funny   b scary   c bored
5. What time do you ___ breakfast?
   a go   b get   c have
6. We can play the football match ___ if it rains.
   a indoors   b in   c on the door
7. The sun is coming out and the temperature is ___ .
   a falling   b rising   c freezing
8. We'll take a ___ so that we can see at night.
   a penknife   b map   c torch
9. Use a ___ to find out which direction we are walking in.
   a torch   b compass   c kit
10. It's good for you to ___ exercise every day.
    a do   b play   c have

Total: 9

Speaking

7 Circle the correct phrase to complete each mini-conversation.

1. **A:** I think small schools are good because the teachers are friendly.
   B: Perhaps you're right / I don't think so. My school is small and the teachers are really friendly.
2. **A:** I think big schools are really noisy.
   B: I think / Maybe, but small schools are often noisy, too!
3. **A:** I reckon it's easier to make friends in a small school.
   B: I suppose so / I don't think so, but I think it's hard to make friends anywhere.
4. **A:** There's more variety of subjects in a big school.
   B: I don't think so. / Yes, that's true. I go to a small school and we can choose from over 20 different subjects.
5. **A:** The sports facilities are better in a big school.
   B: I reckon / I don't agree. A lot of big schools don't have good sports facilities.

Total: 4

Total: 54

Unit 1 Review 15

Get it right! Unit 1

Present simple vs. present continuous: *Wh-* questions

Remember that:
- we use the **present simple** to talk about facts, habits and routines
- we form *Wh-* questions in the **present simple** with *Wh-* + *do/does* + subject + infinitive without *to*. Remember to use *do*.
  ✓ *Where do you go on Saturday mornings?*
  ✗ *Where you go on Saturday mornings?*
- we use the **present continuous** to talk about actions in progress at the time of speaking
- we form *Wh-* questions in the **present continuous** with *Wh-* + *be* + subject + *-ing*. Remember to put *be* before the subject.
  ✓ *What are you doing here today?*
  ✗ *What are you doing here today?*

1 Are the questions correct? Correct the incorrect questions.
1 What you do when it's freezing outside?
   What do you do when it's freezing outside?
2 What do you do at the moment?
   _____
3 Who usually comes to your house at the weekend?
   _____
4 Where your cousin Michael lives?
   _____
5 What are you doing when it snows in your town?
   _____
6 How often you go to school by car?
   _____
7 What James is studying at the moment?
   _____
8 What does time school finishes?
   _____

Past simple vs. past continuous

Remember that:
- we use the **past continuous** (*was/were* + *-ing*) to talk about a long action that was in progress in the past
  ✓ *Sam was jogging when he got lost.*
  ✗ *Sam jogged when he got lost.*
- we use the **past simple** to talk about completed events and actions in the past.
  ✓ *Then suddenly, he realised he was lost.*
  ✗ *Then suddenly, he was realising he was lost.*

2 Find and correct six more mistakes with the past simple and continuous in the email.

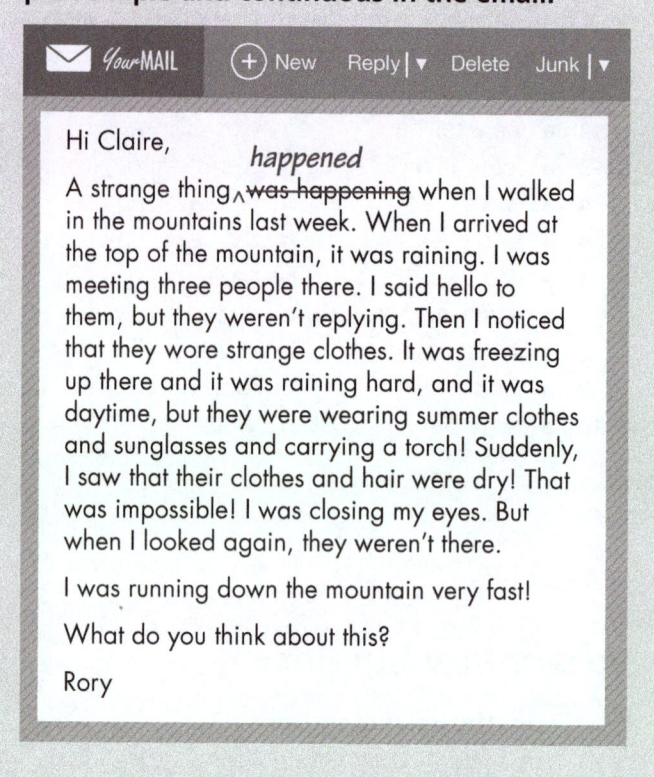

Hi Claire,
                  happened
A strange thing ∧ ~~was happening~~ when I walked in the mountains last week. When I arrived at the top of the mountain, it was raining. I was meeting three people there. I said hello to them, but they weren't replying. Then I noticed that they wore strange clothes. It was freezing up there and it was raining hard, and it was daytime, but they were wearing summer clothes and sunglasses and carrying a torch! Suddenly, I saw that their clothes and hair were dry! That was impossible! I was closing my eyes. But when I looked again, they weren't there.

I was running down the mountain very fast!

What do you think about this?

Rory

Prepositional phrases: time expressions

Remember that:
- we use *in* with months, seasons and years
  ✓ *In June and July, the snow melts.*
  ✓ *Who returned to the island in 1962?*
  ✓ *My class goes on school trips in spring.*
- we use *on* with days of the week and phrases with days of the week
  ✓ *We go to the cinema on Sundays.*
  ✓ *We usually go shopping on Saturday morning.*
- with times of day when the day of the week is not mentioned, we use *in*
  ✓ *It's difficult to see our friends in the evening.*

3 Complete the sentences with *in* or *on*.
1 We often go shopping ___*on*___ Saturday afternoons.
2 _____ July it's usually boiling, but _____ October, we have heavy rain.
3 Are you coming out _____ Friday?
4 What are the average temperatures _____ winter?
5 It's 10.30 _____ the morning and it's sunny.
6 It's sunny and warm _____ spring.

2 A balancing act

Vocabulary

Priorities

1 ★ **Complete the word puzzle with the clues. What is the mystery word?**

1		s	p	o	r	t	s		
2									
3									
4									
5									
6									
7									
8									

1 My friend Matt loves doing ___sports___. He plays football, volleyball and tennis.
2 I go to bed after midnight so I don't get enough _____ .
3 My Mum always says 'With work and family I never have _____ by myself'.
4 I spend a lot of time on the Internet chatting with my friends _____ .
5 My friend Alex draws comics. She loves doing _____ things.
6 Clara loves going to the shopping mall to _____ out with friends.
7 We're going to shop for _____ on Saturday.
8 Everyone helps _____ the house at the weekend. I hate it!

Mystery word: These are all activities that a _____ does.

2 ★ **Match the verbs with the nouns.**

1 competing in
2 hang out
3 doing
4 getting
5 having
6 helping

a time by yourself
b around the house
c something creative
d enough sleep
e sports events
f with friends

3 ★★ **Complete the text with words from Exercises 1 and 2.**

I come from a large family. It's not easy! We all take turns ¹ _helping around the house_ , like washing the floor or cleaning the bathroom. I usually get my older sisters' dresses and jeans when they're too small for them, so I can only dream about ² _____ .

We've only got two computers too, so we don't ³ _____ very often. Also, ⁴ _____ is difficult – there's always something happening with the family. And ⁵ _____ is a problem, because when we go to bed my sisters and I sometimes talk for hours!

Of course I don't always go out with my big sisters, I ⁶ _____ of my own from school. My sisters and I all enjoy painting and drawing, too. ⁷ _____ together is really nice. I also ⁸ _____ . I do athletics and it's great when all my family come to support me! We're all very close!

4 ★★★ **What about you? Write at least five sentences about your priorities. Use vocabulary from Exercises 1 and 2. Explain how you spend your time in the week and at the weekend.**

I don't help around the house in the week, but on Saturday I do.

Language focus 1

should/must

1 ★ Complete the rules in the table.

1	In the affirmative we use should + the _____ .
2	We form negatives with _____ after should.
3	We form questions with should _____ the subject.
4	We use should to say we think something is a _____ idea.

2 ★ Complete the text with should or shouldn't.

My brother and I share a room and we're always fighting. He always says I ¹ _should_ study more before my exams and I ² _____ play computer games all the time. I tell him he ³ _____ leave his clothes on the floor, and that he ⁴ _____ go to bed earlier. Then he says I ⁵ _____ tell him what to do because he's older, and I say he ⁶ _____ have more respect. That's when Mum or Dad usually come in to say we ⁷ _____ stop shouting! ⁸ _____ we stop arguing all the time? I suppose so, but it's fun!

3 ★ Circle the rules in the table.

1	When we make the affirmative, negative and question with must and should, the grammar is **the same / different**.
2	We use the infinitive **with / without** to after must and mustn't.
3	We use must and mustn't to say we think something is **very / not** important.

4 ★★ Complete the sentences with the correct form of must and the verbs in the box.

remember   see   go   help
tell   stay   get up   watch

1 You __must see__ these photos on my phone. They're great!
2 They _____ without us! Tell them to wait.
3 We _____ late on Saturday. We need to catch the bus at 9 o'clock.
4 _____ I _____ around the house now? I'm watching my favourite programme!
5 Joel _____ out late tonight. He's got an important match tomorrow.
6 Why _____ you _____ football all the time? I hate it!
7 You _____ me about your trip to Bogotá.
8 We _____ to text Jenny about the cinema.

5 ★★★ Write sentences with should/shouldn't and must/mustn't and the words in brackets.

1 It's very cold outside. (coat / catch)
   You should wear a coat or you'll catch a cold.
2 I'm sometimes tired in my Maths class. (get / more sleep)
   _____
3 I never remember what homework I have to do. (concentrate)
   _____
4 I've got a really important exam tomorrow. (go to bed / late)
   _____
5 I usually get very hungry before lunch. (snack)
   _____
6 Olivia really wants me to help her. (call / her later)
   _____

Explore verb + noun collocations

6 ★★ Match the sentence halves.

1 Why are you watching
2 I'm hungry! I think I'll
3 You must get
4 I think I'm catching
5 We can't concentrate
6 Tom loves surfing

a in our lesson because there's too much noise.
b TV? Go outside and play!
c the Internet but he should go out more.
d more sleep! You look very tired.
e a cold. I don't feel well.
f have a snack.

18   Unit 2

Listening and vocabulary

Listening

1 ★★ 🔊 **02** Listen to a radio programme discussing how teenagers spend their time. Tick (✓) the things in the list they talk about.
- a studying ✓
- b helping around the house ☐
- c social activities ☐
- d after-school activities ☐
- e holidays ☐
- f homework ☐
- g getting enough sleep ☐
- h clothes and fashion ☐

2 ★★ 🔊 **02** Listen again. Are these sentences true (*T*) or false (*F*)?
1. The discussion topic is what teenagers do at school. _F_
2. Jamie doesn't do any extra activities. ___
3. He usually feels tired. ___
4. The teacher thinks her students do too much. ___
5. She says students should meet every evening to do homework. ___
6. The parent agrees with the teacher. ___
7. He thinks teenagers should concentrate on schoolwork. ___
8. The psychologist agrees with the teenager. ___
9. She thinks being with friends is important. ___
10. She says that helping around the house and sleeping are both important. ___

Performing

3 ★ Complete the text with the words in the box.

> dancing   orchestra   act   voice   play the piano
> ~~on stage~~   microphone   instruments

The concert last night was amazing. From the moment Jake came ¹ _on stage_ everyone in the crowd was shouting, singing and ² _____ . There was a big ³ _____ behind the band and the sound was incredible. Jake took the ⁴ _____ and started singing 'Love is …'. He's got such a powerful ⁵ _____ and all the girls screamed! During the concert he played different ⁶ _____ and for the last song he sat down to ⁷ _____ on his own. And there was a surprise at the end – he told everyone he's going to ⁸ _____ in a film next month. He's a dream!

4 ★★★ Use the words in Exercise 3 to make different words.
1. We often make *microphone* shorter by seven letters. _mic_
2. Add *-al* to this word to describe a piece of music with no singing. _____
3. A person who dances. _____
4. A person who performs in a film or theatre. _____
5. Add *-l* to this word to describe music played by an orchestra. _____
6. A person who plays the piano. _____
7. Change this word to *voc-* and add *-al* and *-ist* for another word for a singer. _____
8. We also use this word as a verb to mean 'put on a performance'. _____

Unit 2   19

Language focus 2

(don't) have to

1 ★ Complete the sentences in the box.

> With *have to* we use ¹_____ or ²_____ to make negatives, and ³_____ or ⁴_____ to make questions.
> After *have/has to* we use the ⁵_____ form of the verb.
> Use *have/has to* to say that it is ⁶_____ to do something.
> Use *don't / doesn't have to* to say that it is not ⁷_____ to do something, but that you ⁸_____ do it if you want.

2 ★ Circle the correct form of *have to* in the sentences.

Fashion ideas: be yourself!

1. It's essential to be yourself. Remember people **have to / don't have to** wear the same clothes as everyone else!
2. You **have to / don't have to** look for clothes or hairstyles which are a bit different.
3. There are a lot of cheap shops, so teenagers **have to / don't have to** spend a lot of money.
4. Everyone **has to / doesn't have to** experiment a little to find their own style.
5. At school we **have to / don't have to** be careful not to look too extreme!
6. You **have to / don't have to** follow fashion. If you don't like it, don't wear it!

3 ★★ Complete the conversation between the PE teacher and a student with the correct form of *have to* and the word in brackets.

A: ¹ *Do I have to be* (I be) really fit to do a triathlon?
B: No, and ² _____ (you be) very good at any of the individual sports.
A: ³ _____ (beginners swim) in open water, like a lake or the sea?
B: No, in all beginner races they swim in a pool.
A: ⁴ _____ (I wear) a helmet for the cycling part?
B: Yes, Every ⁵ _____ (cyclist wear) a helmet to compete.
A: Do I need a racing bicycle?
B: No, ⁶ _____ (your bicycle be) a special one.
A: What about the running part?
B: ⁷ _____ (every competitor wear) a microchip on their shoe, for their official time.
A: Right! Are the rules very complicated?
B: Yes, ⁸ _____ (you read) the rules carefully so you know what to do!

don't have to vs. mustn't

4 ★ Complete the sentences with *don't have to* or *mustn't*.

1. We __*don't have to*__ sing if you don't want to.
2. You _____ use your mobile phone while you're driving.
3. Today's Friday so I _____ do my homework.
4. You _____ forget to say good luck to Dad. He's got a concert tonight.
5. She _____ use a microphone. I can hear her perfectly.
6. She _____ be late for the concert or they won't let her in.

Explore prepositions

5 ★★ Circle the correct words.
1. There's a cinema **in front of** / **above** my uncle's house. You can see it through the window.
2. Don't come in the house **over / until** I tell you to.
3. I try to balance my time **between / near** athletics and homework.
4. We've got a big park **inside / behind** my house.
5. My school is **near / until** our house so I walk to school every day.
6. The party was full **of / over** kids from his school.
7. You must be **until / over** 18 to watch this film.
8. Let's see who's taller. Stand **inside / beside** me and we can see.

6 ★★★ Imagine you are a rich and famous person. How is your imaginary life different from your real life? Write at least five sentences about things you *have to* do now and things you *don't have to* do.

I'm a film star! I don't have to make my bed ...

20 Unit 2

Reading

1 ★ Read about the problems a teenage athlete has. Complete the text with the headings in the box.

> Diet   Schoolwork   ~~The attitude of my friends~~
> Getting enough sleep

BEING A TEENAGE ATHLETE
JUGGLING MY LIFE!   HOME   ABOUT   **BLOG**   CONTACT

I'm a long jumper. I train four times a week and compete on Sundays. I love athletics, but my life isn't easy and involves a lot of *juggling*. Schoolwork, training, family life, sleeping and socialising all need my attention and there are only 24 hours in a day! So what are my biggest problems?

¹ <u>The attitude of my friends</u> : Most of my friends aren't **sporty** so they don't understand why I am. If we're hanging out and I have to leave early because I've got an **athletics meeting** on the next day, they say 'No, Sam, you mustn't go!'

² _____ : An athlete can eat a lot and not get fat, but I must eat healthy food to support all the exercise (and **brainwork**!) I do. I have to ignore the machines selling sweets and chocolate (not easy!) and make sure I eat enormous **helpings** of protein, vegetables and fruit.

³ _____ : When I'm training hard I should go to bed early, or I quickly feel exhausted.

This is a problem, as I've sometimes got **loads of** homework to do when I get home. Luckily, there's Saturday!

⁴ _____ : I have to use every free moment. I often **revise** in the car to and from training. I do homework after dinner, but I shouldn't stay up late, so usually I finish my coursework at the weekend, when my friends are out having fun. I'm not surprised they think I'm crazy!

I don't have to do this, so why do I? Because I'm good at it, and I want to win a gold medal!

2 ★★ Complete the sentences with the words in the box. Use the words in **bold** in the text to help you.

> athletics meeting   revise   ~~loads of~~   helping (noun)
> brainwork   ignore   juggling   sporty

1 Another phrase for *lots of* is ____loads of____ .
2 If you _____ something, you act like it's not happening.
3 An _____ is an event where people compete in sports like running or jumping.
4 If you like playing sports you are a _____ person.
5 A _____ is a portion of food.
6 You have to think a lot when you do _____ .
7 To keep throwing three or four balls in the air, without dropping them is called _____ .
8 To _____ before an exam you read things you did in class and try to remember them.

3 ★★ Choose the correct answers.
1 How many times a week does Sam do athletics training?
   a five times a week
   b four times a week
2 Why can he eat a lot?
   a he does a lot of 'brainwork'
   b he doesn't get fat
3 What happens when he does a lot of training and he doesn't go to bed early?
   a he feels tired very quickly
   b he can't compete on Saturdays
4 How do Sam's friends feel about him?
   a they think he has fun
   b they think he's crazy

4 ★★★ Write rules for Sam's life. Use *should/ shouldn't*, *must/mustn't* and *has to/doesn't have to* and the words in the box.

> do homework   eat sweets and chocolate
> go to parties   eat a lot of protein
> stay up late   ~~train four times a week~~

1 *Sam has to train four times a week.*
2 _____
3 _____
4 _____
5 _____
6 _____

Unit 2   21

Writing

A competition entry

1 Read Mike's competition entry. Did he enjoy the camp?

WIN A VIDEO GAME

Write a review of an experience where you learned something new from using a computer. The best review will win a free video game!

Competition entry:

I love computer games, so I learned a lot from the two-week 'Game Design Summer Camp' I did this year. Everyone should try [1] _it_ ! There were loads of [2] _____ to choose from. My [3] _____ were the talks by professional game designers, and the gaming tournaments in the evenings and at weekends. And every afternoon we had outdoor activities, like swimming and volleyball. But the most important [4] _____ was designing a 3D video game. I did [5] _____ with my friends Carla and Sam – our instructors helped, of course! On the last day when we finished our games we had to present [6] _____ to a group of experts.

I was terrified, but [7] _____ were really nice. What did I learn? I learned how computer games work and I also learned how to do a good presentation. Not bad!

Mike

2 Read the competition entry again and match the questions with the answers.
1 What was the camp about? _c_
2 When was it? ___
3 How did Mike learn about computer games? ___
4 What did they do in the evenings and at weekends? ___
5 What activities were there in the afternoon? ___
6 Who did he design a game with? ___
7 What did they do at the end of the course? ___
8 What did Mike think of the course? ___

a His friends Carla and Sam.
b There was information from professionals.
c How to design computer games.
d In the summer.
e They presented their game to experts.
f It was amazing.
g Sports and outdoor activities.
h Compete in computer games.

Useful language Avoiding repetition (1)

3 Complete Mike's competition entry with the words in the box.

| it | this | activities | favourites | one | them | they |

4 Rewrite the sentences to avoid repetition. Use the text in Exercise 1 to help you.
1 I went to an amazing summer camp. The camp was about performing and acting.
I went to an amazing summer camp. It was about performing and acting.
2 There were lots of activities but my favourite activities were juggling and singing.
_____
3 I sang a song and then my friend sang a song by One Direction.
_____
4 We tried juggling but juggling is really difficult.
_____
5 There were big helpings of vegetables but I didn't eat the helpings of vegetables.
_____
6 All the students on the camp were the same age as me and all the students were really good actors.
_____

22 — Unit 2

Writing

5 Complete the sentences with the correct prepositions.
1. There were loads ___of___ activities to try.
2. We had a chance to hang out _____ people from different countries.
3. Sailing camp was perfect _____ me.
4. You choose _____ six activities.
5. At night we sat _____ a fire singing.
6. We went into town to shop _____ souvenirs.

> **WRITING TIP**
> Make it better! ✓ ✓ ✓
> Use time expressions but be careful with articles and prepositions.

6 Choose the correct time expressions.
1. We played basketball **in** / (**in the**) afternoons.
2. There were different activities **at** / **in the** night.
3. Most people went home **in** / **at** weekends.
4. The activities finished **at** / **to** 4 o'clock.
5. **On** / **In** the first day, we got into groups.
6. They put on films **at every night** / **every night**.

> **WRITING TIP**
> Make it better! ✓ ✓ ✓
> Use transition words to join sentences and ideas.

7 Complete the competition entry with the words in the box.

> of course   And then   Actually
> ~~In fact~~   So far   For instance

> Before I went to surf camp last summer, I didn't like the sea. ¹___In fact___, I hated it! However, the camp was amazing and, ²_____ I had a great time. There were lots of activities. ³_____, you could try windsurfing or kitesurfing. ⁴_____ if you didn't want to go in the water, you could learn about surfboards. ⁵_____ surfboards are difficult to take care of. ⁶_____ it's the best camp I've been on.

8 Read the competition entry again. Tick (✓) the things in the list that Mike writes about.
- the daytime/night/weekend activities ☐
- the instructors / other campers ☐
- the daily routine ☐
- why you liked it ☐
- the food ☐
- the weather ☐

PLAN

9 Read about the competition in the box. Use the headings in Exercise 8 or your own ideas to make notes.

> **ACTIVITY CAMP COMPETITION**
>
> **Win a FREE activity camp for two weeks!**
>
> Write about an activity camp that you went to. What sort of camp was it? The best description will win two weeks at the best activity camp in the world!

WRITE

10 Write your competition entry. Look at page 27 of the Student's Book to help you.

_____
_____
_____
_____
_____
_____
_____
_____
_____
_____
_____
_____
_____
_____
_____

CHECK

11 Check your writing. Can you say YES to these questions?
- Is there any repetition in your competition entry?
- Do you use transition words between ideas and sentences?
- Are the prepositions correct?
- Do you use time expressions correctly?
- Are the spelling and punctuation correct?

Do you need to write a second draft?

2 Review

Vocabulary
Priorities

1 Match the phrases with the examples.

1 chatting with friends online
2 hanging out with friends
3 shopping for clothes
4 helping around the house
5 getting enough sleep
6 having time for yourself
7 doing something creative
8 doing sports

a going to bed early
b using Facebook or Twitter to send messages to friends
c going to a café to be with your friends
d buying new shoes and jeans
e playing for your school basketball team
f reading a book in your room
g designing computer games
h cleaning your room and doing the washing-up

Total: 7

Performing

2 Put the letters in brackets in order to make words.

1 I can't hear you. Could you speak into the ___microphone___ ? (poochminer)
2 To work on the radio, you have to have a nice _____ . (icove).
3 He always gets very nervous before he goes on _____ . (gsate).
4 Listening to an _____ live is amazing. (aeothsrcr)
5 We're going _____ on Friday. (gnadinc)
6 OK, you can sing and dance. But can you _____ ? (tca)
7 She played all the _____ on her last album. (ssmettinnur)
8 My grandmother plays the _____ and she's 85. (oniap)

Total: 7

Language focus
should/must

3 Complete the letters with *should* or *shouldn't*.

Dear Abby,
I have problems getting enough sleep. My parents say I ¹ _should_ go to bed earlier. My best friend told me I ² _____ eat so much chocolate. My sister says I ³ _____ listen to relaxing music before I go to bed. What do you think? What ⁴ _____ I do?
'Worried'

Dear 'Worried',
There are many reasons for not getting enough sleep. You ⁵ _____ worry about it, because worrying can keep you awake. You also ⁶ _____ eat dinner late, and you ⁷ _____ try drinking some herbal tea before you go to bed.
Abby

Total: 6

4 Match the sentences and complete them with *must* or *mustn't*.

1 You look so tired.
2 You look hungry.
3 You're really late!
4 It's Mum's birthday tomorrow.
5 The concert is at 6 pm.
6 I need to finish my Science project.

a You _____ eat some lunch.
b You _____ hurry!
c I _____ forget to buy her a card.
d We _____ be late.
e You _mustn't_ go to bed late.
f I _____ do it this weekend.

Total: 5

(don't) have to vs. mustn't

5 Complete the sentences. Use *don't have to*, *doesn't have to* or *mustn't*.

1 At my school you _don't have to_ wear a uniform.
2 Be careful, you _____ drop the glasses!
3 My brother is only four years old, so he _____ help around the house.
4 On Sundays we _____ get up early.
5 Tomorrow I have PE at school, so I _____ forget to bring my sports clothes.

Total: 4

Language builder

6 Circle the correct options.

Gina: What ¹___ last weekend?
Alex: I ²___ my dog for a long walk. How about you?
Gina: I ³___ a marathon. But when we ⁴___ , it ⁵___ to rain and we all got wet!
Alex: Oh, dear! ⁶___ every day?
Gina: Before running a marathon, I ⁷___ every morning.
Alex: Wow! You ⁸___ tired sometimes. ⁹___ eat a special diet?
Gina: Not really, I just eat lots of vegetables and fruit and I ¹⁰___ eat sweets or chocolates. Do you want to go running with me?
Alex: OK. But first I ¹¹___ to find my running shoes!

1	ⓐ	did you do	b	you did do	c	you did
2	a	was taking	b	took	c	take
3	a	running	b	was running	c	ran
4	a	were running	b	ran	c	run
5	a	start	b	was starting	c	started
6	a	Do you run	b	You do run	c	You run
7	a	run usually	b	usually running	c	usually run
8	a	must feel	b	should feel	c	did
9	a	You have to	b	You do have to	c	Do you have to
10	a	mustn't	b	don't have to	c	'm not eating
11	a	must	b	should	c	have

Total: 10

Vocabulary builder

7 Circle the correct options.
1 It was cold, so the rain turned into ___ .
   ⓐ hail   b thunder   c heat wave
2 Sing into the ___ . I can't hear you.
   a piano   b microphone   c orchestra
3 It was -3 °C – the temperature was below ___ .
   a freezing   b boiling   c lightning
4 I study all the time. ___ is so important.
   a Fashion   b Education   c Transport
5 When you cross the road you need to look ___ both directions.
   a of   b on   c in
6 We need to take a ___ because it will be dark at night.
   a compass   b torch   c camera
7 Pack a ___ because it can be cold at night.
   a sleeping bag   b water bottle   c map
8 I like sports ___ , like football and tennis matches.
   a games   b networks   c events
9 I don't usually stay ___ late at the weekend.
   a on   b out   c after
10 That new film is really scary – I was ___ .
   a terrified   b stressed   c exhausted

Total: 9

Speaking

8 Put the words in the correct order to make phrases for helping someone to do something.
1 show / Let / you / me
   Let me show you.
2 know / you / to / it / how / Do / do ?
   ___
3 good / very / at / not / I'm / Maths
   ___
4 hand / give / you / I'll / a / like / you / if
   ___
5 kind / really / That / 's
   ___
6 very / It / really / simple / 's
   ___

Total: 5

Total: 53

Get it right! Unit 2

should/must

Remember that:
- we use the infinitive without *to* after *should/shouldn't* and *must/mustn't*
  - ✓ You shouldn't go to bed late the night before an exam.
  - ✗ You shouldn't ~~to~~ go to bed late the night before an exam.

1 Find and correct five more mistakes with *should* and *must* in the rules.

IF THERE IS A FIRE IN YOUR HOME …

1. You mustn't ~~to~~ panic! You should concentrate and breathe slowly.
2. You should to make sure everybody in the house is awake.
3. You must leave the house as quickly as possible.
4. If you can see smoke under the door, you mustn't to open it.
5. If the door is hot, you must to find another way to leave.
6. You should find a door that goes to the outside.
7. When you are out of the house, you must to telephone for help.
8. You shouldn't to go back into the house for any reason.

have to

Remember that:
- we don't usually use the contracted form of *have* with *have to*
  - ✓ On Saturdays, I have to help with the shopping.
  - ✗ On Saturdays, I've to help with the shopping.
- we use the infinitive without *to* after *(don't) have to*
  - ✓ I have to look after my younger brother.
  - ✗ I have to ~~looking~~ after my younger brother.
  - ✗ I have to ~~looked~~ after my younger brother.
- we use *have* after *I/you/we/they*, and *has* after *he/she/it*
  - ✓ My grandmother has to go to the hospital.
  - ✗ My grandmother ~~have~~ to go to the hospital.

2 Find and correct six more mistakes with *have to* in the email.

> Hi Lucy,
>
> I'm sorry I can't hang out with you tomorrow 😞. ~~I've~~ **I have** to do so many things before school starts again on Monday! Tomorrow morning I have to going shopping for new shoes for school. Then, I have to took my brother to the dentist. He have to be there at 12 o'clock. My mum can't take him because she have to work. This afternoon I've to help around the house because my grandparents are coming to visit. I have to spent all weekend with them! 😞 I don't really mind, but I never have any time by myself!
>
> I have to go now.
>
> Bye!
>
> Claire

need to

- we use the infinitive with *to* after *need*
  - ✓ I need to be alone sometimes.
  - ✗ I ~~need be~~ alone sometimes.
  - ✗ I ~~need being~~ alone sometimes.

3 Circle the correct option.
1. There are three things you need **remember** / **(to remember)** for the exam.
2. To get to sleep, you need **to feel** / **feeling** relaxed.
3. You really need **catch** / **to catch** up on your sleep. You're studying too hard.
4. You need **doing** / **to do** more exercise.
5. Teenagers need **to get** / **get** at least eight hours of sleep every night.
6. I need **to help** / **helping** my dad tomorrow.

3 Art all around us

Vocabulary
Art around us

1 ★ Put the letters in order to make words connected with the arts.

rotcenc lalh   kurbse   rejglug   vlinig usteat
troipart intreap   raygell   laurm   fatigrif
ebnithoxii   rutspluce

1 _concert hall_   6 _____
2 _____   7 _____
3 _____   8 _____
4 _____   9 _____
5 _____   10 _____

2 ★ Write the vocabulary from Exercise 1 in the correct place.
1 Two buildings used for the arts:
   concert hall, _____
2 Three people you see in the street:
   _____
3 Two things you can see on an outside wall:
   _____
4 Two things you see in a gallery:
   _____
5 A person who paints people: _____

3 ★★ Complete the sentences. Use vocabulary from Exercise 1.
1 My school had a lot of ugly _graffiti_ on the outside wall, so they asked the students to paint a(n) _____ instead.
2 The Picasso _____ in Berlin this summer is very popular. It's difficult to get tickets.
3 There are often _____ in the New York subway. People like hearing music in the stations.
4 The Ramblas in Barcelona is famous for its _____ _____ . They don't move for hours.
5 We've got a(n) _____ _____ in my town but it's all classical music, so I don't go.
6 The Louvre is a museum and art _____ in Paris.

4 ★★ Read the clues and write the words.
1 These can be music students who need money.   _buskers_
2 These can be metal, stone or plastic.   _____
3 They need to practise so things don't fall.   _____
4 You usually have to pay for music here.   _____
5 This person often copies a photo of someone.   _____
6 This often lasts for several months.   _____

5 ★★★ Write answers to the questions.
1 Which of the things on this page _haven't_ you got where you live?
2 What do you think of graffiti?
3 What kind of street performers do you watch?
4 Have you got any paintings at home? What are they of?

Unit 3   27

Language focus 1

Present perfect for indefinite past time

1 ★ Circle the correct options.
1. Famous musicians like Bob Dylan, Paul McCartney and Bon Jovi **have performed** / has performed as buskers (but they didn't make a lot of money!).
2. That juggler **is dropped / has dropped** a ball every time I **'ve watched / 'm watched** him perform. He isn't very good!
3. Alan **never has enjoyed / has never enjoyed** going to exhibitions of classical paintings.
4. Sometimes living statues suddenly move. It surprises you if you **haven't to notice / haven't noticed** them before.
5. A local youth group **has painted / is paint** several murals on the outside of the cultural centre.

2 ★★ Complete the sentences with the correct form of the verbs in the box. Use the present perfect affirmative or negative.

meet   take   win   see   be   ~~speak~~

1. We ____have spoken____ to the teachers about painting a mural in the dining room at school.
2. My parents _____ me to any galleries so I _____ a lot of art.
3. One Dutch man _____ the living statues World Championships three times.
4. She works in a record company so she _____ a lot of musicians.
5. My favourite bands _____ to my town because we haven't got a concert hall.

3 ★★ Complete the text with the present perfect form of the verbs in brackets.
Banksy, the world famous graffiti artist, is a mystery man. He ¹ _has never revealed_ (never reveal) his real name and ² _____ (create) murals all over the world. Banksy paints quickly so the police ³ _____ (never catch) him. He's a street artist, but people ⁴ _____ (buy) his work for thousands of pounds. He ⁵ _____ (paint) portraits too, like Kate Moss and Queen Victoria (now owned by Christina Aguilera). Banksy ⁶ _____ (make) a lot of money from his art, and his work ⁷ _____ (increase) interest in street art in general.

4 ★★★ Write at least five sentences about your experiences with art and music. Use the words in the box or your own ideas, and verbs in the present perfect.

| see an art exhibition   paint a mural |
| go to a concert hall   see living statues |
| paint graffiti   give money to a busker |

Explore collocations

5 ★★ Complete the sentences with the words in the box.

make   posted   ~~taking~~   about   at   hard

1. Maddy has always liked ____taking____ photos.
2. I've never been very good _____ painting.
3. We made a funny video and I've _____ it online.
4. My mum and dad work very _____. They're both doctors.
5. Our teacher is really passionate _____ opera. She always plays music in class.
6. I don't think the most important thing in life is to _____ money.

28 Unit 3

Listening and vocabulary

Instruments

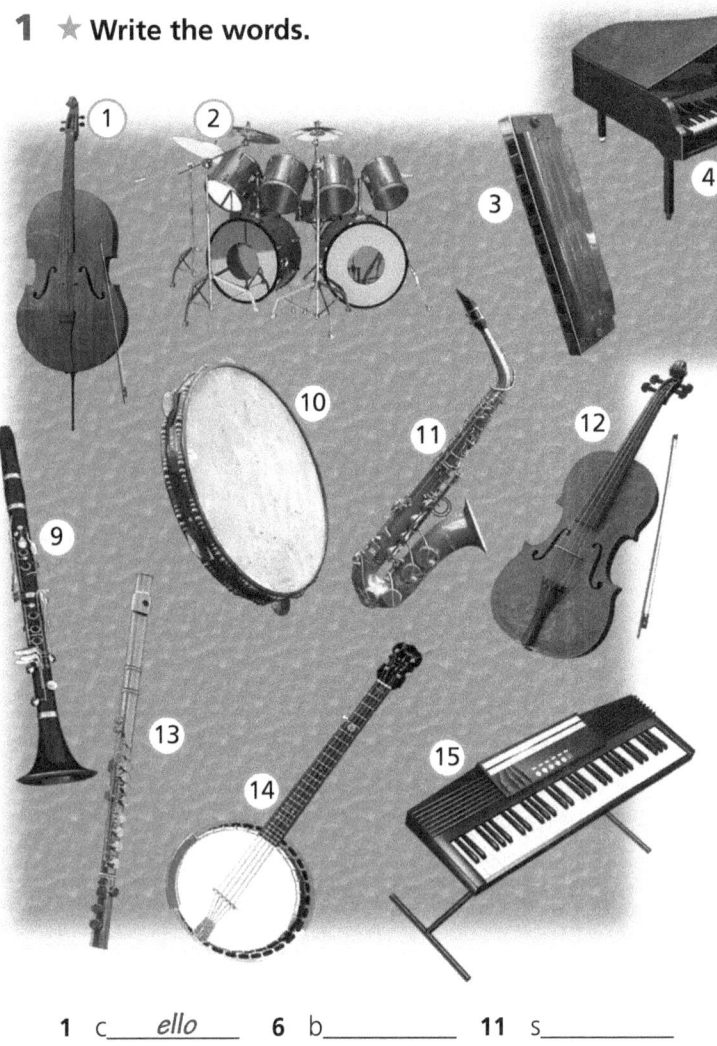

1 ★ Write the words.

1 c _ello_	6 b_____	11 s_____
2 d_____	7 r_____	12 v_____
3 m_____	8 t_____	13 f_____
o_____	9 c_____	14 b_____
4 p_____	10 t_____	15 k_____
5 g_____		

2 ★★ Answer the questions with words from Exercise 1. Not all the words are needed.

1 Which instruments can you find in a rock band?
keyboards, _____

2 Which instruments do children often play in primary school?
_____

3 Which instruments are often played in jazz?
_____

4 Which instruments can you see in an orchestra?
_____

5 Which instruments are difficult to play in the street?
_____

Listening

3 ★ 🔊 03 Listen to a radio interview with two street performers. What do they do?

> living statue   juggler   jazz musician
> magician   fire-eater   bongo-drummer

Greg is a _____ and **Alice** is a _____ .

4 ★ 🔊 03 Listen again. (Circle) the correct options.

1 Greg decided to do his job when he was **fifteen** / **(sixteen)**.
2 He first thought of doing it at a **music festival** / **street carnival**.
3 He **was** / **wasn't** a good magician when he first started.
4 He's performed **only in Europe** / **in many different countries**.
5 He likes **the lifestyle** / **lots of people watching him**.
6 Alice thinks juggling with fire **is** / **isn't** dangerous.
7 She has worked in a **circus school** / **circus**.
8 She **always** / **sometimes** works at night.
9 She can make a lot of money **in a short time** / **at night**.
10 There are **a lot of** / **a few** women street performers in Covent Garden.

Unit 3   29

Language focus 2

Present perfect with ever/never

1 ★ Circle the correct options.
1 I have **ever** / **never** given money to a busker.
2 Have you **ever** / **never** tried to juggle?
3 My dad **has played never** / **has never played** the piano.
4 Tanya **has never seen** / **never has seen** a living statue.
5 **Has your teacher ever** / **Has ever your teacher** taken you to a gallery?
6 I **never have** / **have never** been to that concert hall.

2 ★★ Put the words in order to make questions and sentences.
1 your family/ made / you / for / Have / ever / dinner / ?
   Have you ever made dinner for your family?
2 visited / ever / the Tate Gallery / they / Have / ?
   _____
3 ever / she / Has / a live concert / seen / ?
   _____
4 never / a famous person. / met / She's
   _____
5 never / that book. / read / I've
   _____
6 helped / me. / never / You've
   _____

3 ★ Write present perfect questions and the correct answers. ✓ = yes and ✗ = no.
1 your friend / ever / listen to / an opera? ✓
   Has your friend ever listened to an opera?
   Yes, she has.
2 your parents / ever / go to / a music festival? ✗
   _____
3 she / hear / of the escape artist Houdini? ✗
   _____
4 the students / finish / their art project? ✓
   _____
5 you and your friends / ever / see / a famous band? ✓
   _____
6 you / listen to / their new CD? ✗
   _____

4 ★★★ Write answers to the questions. Use the present perfect.
1 What exhibitions have you been to?
   _____
2 Has anyone you know ever performed in public?
   _____
3 What TV series have you followed?
   _____
4 What famous bands have you seen?
   _____
5 What creative things have you done?
   _____

I've been to a modern art exhibition, a street art exhibition, …

Explore phrasal verbs with up

5 ★★ Match the sentence halves.
1 My mum says I can't go out — **d**
2 They pressed the button — ___
3 We missed the start of the film — ___
4 The photographer set up his camera — ___
5 We had a party — ___
6 We can't have dinner — ___

a and started taking photos.
b because Jacob showed up late.
c and we all dressed up as superheroes.
d until I tidy up my room.
e because Adam hasn't picked up the food.
f and thousands of small lights lit up the streets.

Reading

1 ★ Read the text about being a living statue. Is it a difficult job?

Being a LIVING STATUE

Nowadays you see living statues all over the world. They wear elaborate **costumes** and body paint, and stand without moving for hours. But what's it like? Is it difficult? I spoke to Nina, a living statue in London.

'You need to be physically and mentally **fit**. It's actually quite hard standing **still**, and you have to eat before you start or you feel ill.

'We wear body paint so we look like real metal or **stone** statues. Metallic paint takes over an hour to put on and it's difficult to **get off**, too. Every week I have a sauna to clean my skin. I love designing different costumes and being creative. We even paint our clothes to make them look heavy. In the winter you need to wear thermal underwear under your costume so you don't **shiver** with cold.

'I've worked at glamorous birthday parties for famous people, and in parks in the rain, and I've just been to the World Championships in Holland. There were 300 statues and 300,000 visitors. It was incredible! Most people love us but sometimes young children are frightened and I've seen one or two cry!'

Antonio Santos from Barcelona holds the world record for standing still, an incredible 20 hours, 11 minutes and 38 seconds, but the longest Nina has stood without moving is two and a half hours, at a party. 'It was awful! So now, I move. If someone gives me money, I **blow a kiss** or do a dance to say thank you. And of course if you need to **sneeze** or something, you have to 'come alive' and make it part of the performance. It's hard work but fun!'

2 ★★ Complete the sentences with the words in the box. Use the words in **bold** in the text to help you.

| blow a kiss   sneeze   costume   ~~stone~~   get off |
| shiver   fit [adjective]   still [adjective] |

1 That ___stone___ flowerpot looks great but it's really heavy.
2 Did he wear a pirate _____ for Carnival?
3 Oh! I want to _____ but I can't. It's a horrible feeling.
4 I always _____ to my granny when we leave her house to drive home.
5 I think this paint on my T-shirt is permanent. It's impossible to _____ .
6 My cousin is very active. She can't sit _____ for one minute.
7 It was freezing outside and we started to _____ .
8 My mum goes running to stay _____ .

3 ★★ Read the text again. Are these sentences true (*T*) or false (*F*)? Correct the false sentences.

1 You can only see living statues in Europe. F
   They are all over the world.
2 Living statues need to use their mind and their body.
   _____
3 The paint is easy to put on and get off.
   _____
4 Nina works in lots of different places.
   _____
5 Lots of people are scared of the living statues.
   _____
6 Nina doesn't enjoy her job.
   _____

4 ★★★ Read the sentences. Tick (✓) the ones a living statue probably says. What does the other person do?

1 'I'm wearing three T-shirts under my costume – it's really cold.' ✓
2 'I sometimes drop a ball when I try with six.' ☐
3 'A little girl started crying when she saw me.' ☐
4 'A bird landed on my head today.' ☐
5 'Sometimes I stand on one leg and do it with three knives.' ☐
6 'I'm going for a sauna now to wash the paint off.' ☐

5 ★★★ Imagine working as a living statue. What is good about it? What are the difficult things? Write your ideas.

Unit 3   31

Writing

An Internet post

1 Read Pete's Internet post. How many different types of performers does he write about?

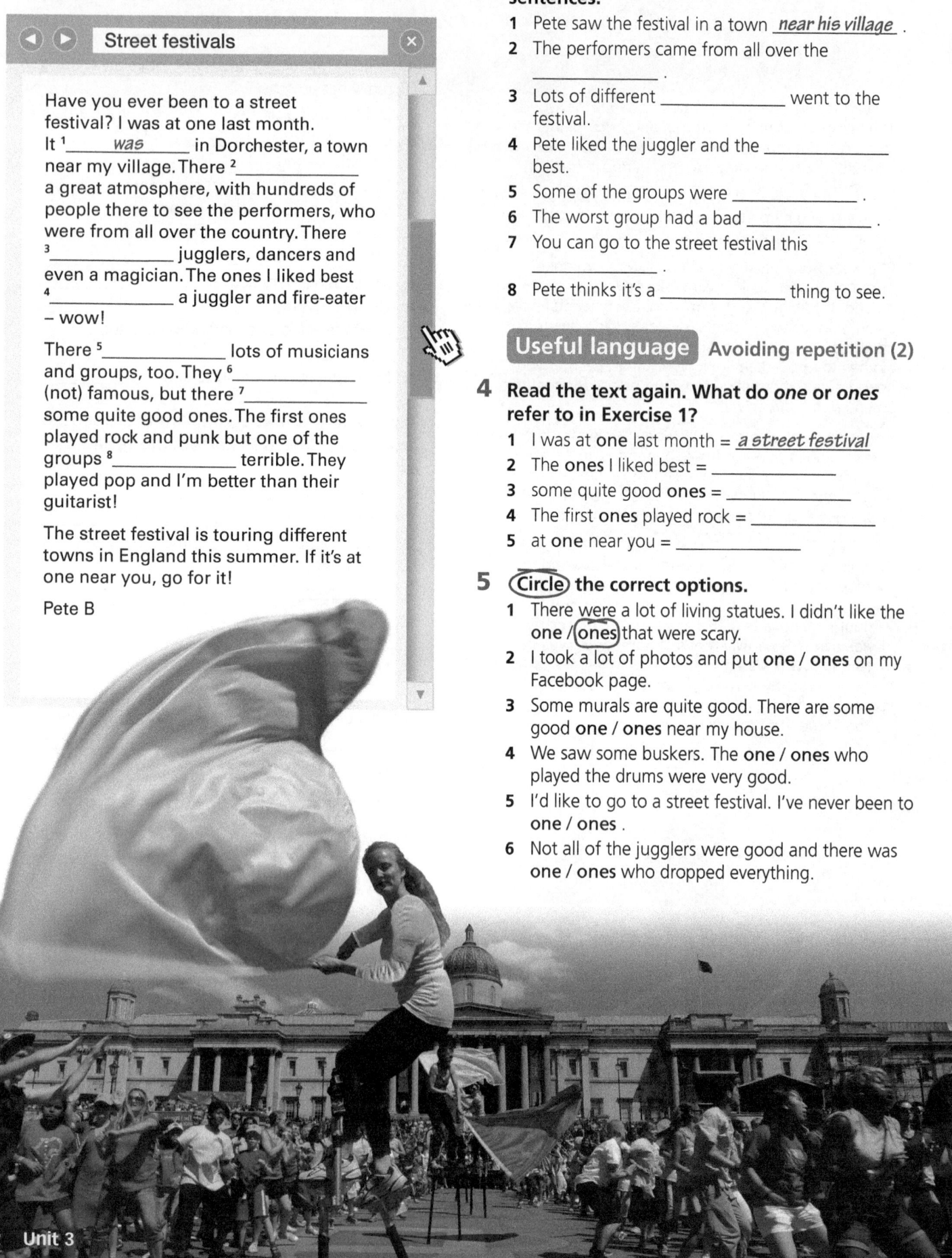

Street festivals

Have you ever been to a street festival? I was at one last month. It ¹___was___ in Dorchester, a town near my village. There ²_____ a great atmosphere, with hundreds of people there to see the performers, who were from all over the country. There ³_____ jugglers, dancers and even a magician. The ones I liked best ⁴_____ a juggler and fire-eater – wow!

There ⁵_____ lots of musicians and groups, too. They ⁶_____ (not) famous, but there ⁷_____ some quite good ones. The first ones played rock and punk but one of the groups ⁸_____ terrible. They played pop and I'm better than their guitarist!

The street festival is touring different towns in England this summer. If it's at one near you, go for it!

Pete B

2 Complete the Internet post with the correct forms of the verb *be*.

3 Read the Internet post again. Complete the sentences.
1 Pete saw the festival in a town _near his village_.
2 The performers came from all over the _____.
3 Lots of different _____ went to the festival.
4 Pete liked the juggler and the _____ best.
5 Some of the groups were _____.
6 The worst group had a bad _____.
7 You can go to the street festival this _____.
8 Pete thinks it's a _____ thing to see.

Useful language Avoiding repetition (2)

4 Read the text again. What do *one* or *ones* refer to in Exercise 1?
1 I was at **one** last month = _a street festival_
2 The **ones** I liked best = _____
3 some quite good **ones** = _____
4 The first **ones** played rock = _____
5 at **one** near you = _____

5 Circle the correct options.
1 There were a lot of living statues. I didn't like the one / **ones** that were scary.
2 I took a lot of photos and put one / ones on my Facebook page.
3 Some murals are quite good. There are some good one / ones near my house.
4 We saw some buskers. The one / ones who played the drums were very good.
5 I'd like to go to a street festival. I've never been to one / ones.
6 Not all of the jugglers were good and there was one / ones who dropped everything.

Writing

6 Rewrite the sentences. Put the words in brackets in the correct place.

1. There were buskers and there were some amazing jugglers. (too)
   <u>There were buskers and there were some amazing jugglers, too.</u>

2. There was a busker who played 10 different instruments! (even)
   _____
   _____

3. We went to an exhibition and we saw some portrait painters. (also)
   _____
   _____

4. I've seen a busker who played the mouth organ. (never)
   _____
   _____

5. Have you seen a street magician? (ever)
   _____
   _____

7 Circle the correct options.

1. He was **the more amazing** / **the most amazing** juggler I've ever seen.
2. I'm a **better** / **best** keyboard player than him!
3. I've never seen a **worse** / **worst** living statue!
4. The busker I liked **better** / **best** was a young girl who played the saxophone.
5. He dressed up as a sheep – it was the **funnier** / **funniest** costume I've ever seen.
6. I've never seen a **better** / **best** portrait.

> **WRITING TIP**
> Make it better! ✓ ✓ ✓
> Make a recommendation at the end of your Internet post to the reader.

8 Read the sentences. Which one is <u>not</u> a recommendation?

1. If it comes to your town, go for it!
2. The exhibition is amazing. You shouldn't miss it!
3. I think everybody should go and see this festival.
4. There were lots of great things to do.
5. When it comes to your town, you can't miss it!

9 Put the information in the order it appears in the Internet post in Exercise 1.

> the audience   the performers
> writer's opinion of artists   ~~where it was~~
> favourite performer   recommendation

1. <u>where it was</u>
2. _____
3. _____
4. _____
5. _____
6. _____

PLAN

10 Invent a street festival. Make notes for each heading in Exercise 9.

WRITE

11 Write an Internet post about your festival. Look at page 39 of the Student's Book to help you.

_____
_____
_____
_____
_____
_____
_____
_____
_____
_____
_____
_____
_____
_____
_____

CHECK

12 Check your writing. Can you say YES to these questions?

- Is the information from Exercise 9 in your description?
- Do you use *one* or *ones* to avoid repetition?
- Do you use comparatives and superlatives correctly?
- Are words like *too*, *even*, *ever*, *also* and *never* in the correct place in the sentences?
- Do you make a recommendation at the end?
- Are the spelling and punctuation correct?

Do you need to write a second draft?

3 Review

Vocabulary
Art around us

1 Circle the correct options.
1. A busker plays music ___ .
   a on the street   b in a concert hall
2. A portrait painter paints pictures of ___ .
   a people   b places
3. You usually see graffiti in ___ .
   a the street   b a museum
4. A juggler ___ .
   a makes paintings and sculptures
   b throws and catches objects
5. You can listen to music in ___ .
   a a concert hall   b a gallery
6. You go to a gallery to see ___ .
   a an exhibition   b a concert
7. The ___ moved because I gave it money.
   a juggler   b living statue
8. The grey wall was boring, so we painted ___ .
   a a mural   b an exhibition

Total: 7

Instruments

2 Put the letters in order to make musical instruments.
1. ratuig — *guitar*
2. drcerore — _____
3. Interica — _____
4. poxeshano — _____
5. niolvi — _____
6. murtept — _____
7. bronautemi — _____
8. leutf — _____
9. ngobso — _____
10. roasbdyke — _____

Total: 9

Language focus
Present perfect for indefinite past time

3 Match the sentence halves.
1. She's never performed
2. My brother has worked as
3. I'm sorry but I haven't finished
4. I haven't noticed
5. They've painted a
6. We've watched

a my homework.
b mural outside the library.
c in public before.
d any graffiti where I live.
e all the Harry Potter films.
f a busker in New York.

Total: 5

4 Complete the text with the present perfect form of the verbs in brackets.

I ¹'ve always ___wanted___ (want) to have a band and now I do. I ²_____ (ask) some friends to join, too. Mark ³_____ (play) the guitar with two other bands. Julie ⁴_____ (never sing) with a band, but she's got a fantastic voice. We ⁵_____ (not give) any concerts, but we ⁶_____ (practise) a lot. We ⁷_____ (begin) to write some songs and we ⁸_____ (send) a demo recording to some music companies!

Total: 7

Present perfect with *ever/never*

5 Write present perfect sentences and questions with *ever* and *never*.
1. I / see / a famous band ✗
   I've never seen a famous band.
2. you / be / to a concert?
   _____
3. your brother / meet / a famous person?
   _____
4. they / be / to Russia ✗
   _____
5. she / eat / meat?
   _____
6. we / see / the sea ✗
   _____

Total: 5

UNIT 3

Language builder

6 Complete the conversation with the missing words. Circle the correct options.

Isabel: ¹___ played any musical instruments?
John: Yes, I ²___ to play the banjo.
Isabel: That's interesting. I ³___ the banjo.
John: I ⁴___ to a music festival last year. Some buskers ⁵___ the banjo and I liked the sound.
Isabel: Is it difficult?
John: Not really, but you ⁶___ to practise every day.
Isabel: I want to learn a musical instrument, too. What ⁷___ play?
John: Well, first you ⁸___ decide what kind of music you want to play.
Isabel: I want to play rock music. I ⁹___ of buying drums but they're very expensive. And ¹⁰___ find a teacher?
John: You ¹¹___ do that now – you can practise by yourself first.

1	**a** Have you ever	**b** Did you	**c** Were you
2	**a** learn	**b** 'm learning	**c** did learn
3	**a** 've never tried	**b** never have tried	**c** 've tried never
4	**a** go	**b** was going	**c** went
5	**a** have played	**b** were playing	**c** are playing
6	**a** mustn't	**b** should	**c** have
7	**a** I should	**b** should I	**c** do I should
8	**a** should	**b** shouldn't	**c** have
9	**a** think	**b** thought	**c** was thinking
10	**a** have I to	**b** I do have to	**c** do I have to
11	**a** don't have to	**b** not have to	**c** mustn't

Total: 10

Vocabulary builder

7 Circle the correct options.

1 It's freezing outside. You'll ___ a cold.
   a take   **b** catch   **c** make
2 It's very dark. Have you got a ___ ?
   a torch   **b** map   **c** penknife
3 There was a huge ___ on the wall with lots of colours.
   a busker   **b** exhibition   **c** mural
4 Abby was afraid of the ___ and lightning.
   a hail   **b** snowstorm   **c** thunder
5 Before you go out in the sun put on some ___ .
   a sun cream   **b** glasses   **c** conditions
6 You should help ___ the house and tidy your room.
   a for   **b** around   **c** through
7 We'll wait ___ Lily comes.
   a near   **b** over   **c** until
8 A ___ is like a big violin.
   a cello   **b** clarinet   **c** piano
9 There were about 200 people ___ total.
   a on   **b** to   **c** in
10 I waited at the cinema for an hour and he never ___ up.
   a picked   **b** set   **c** showed

Total: 9

Speaking

8 Put the sentences in the correct order to make a conversation.

___ **Sally:** How about meeting at my house at 6.30?
___ **Lynn:** OK. See you later.
___ **Sally:** Yeah, why not?
_1_ **Lynn:** Do you fancy going out for pizza later?
___ **Lynn:** I can't meet until 7, sorry.
___ **Sally:** Sounds good! Shall I ask my dad to pick you up?
___ **Lynn:** What time shall we meet then?

Total: 6

Total: 58

Unit 3 Review   35

Get it right! Unit 3

Present perfect with been/gone

1 Find and correct three more mistakes with **been** and **gone**.

I wanted to have a party on Saturday, but no one can come! Mary has ~~been~~ *gone* to London with her family, so she can't come. Paul has gone to France for two weeks and isn't coming back until next Friday. Clara has gone skiing, so she can't come. And I don't know about Tia. I've gone to her house, but there was no one home. Maybe she's gone to visit her grandparents. I phoned Leonardo and he hasn't been anywhere, but he's ill in bed at home! Even my brother has been on holiday until next week. I think I'm going to have to have my party another day!

Present perfect with ever/never

Remember that:
- we use **ever** in present perfect questions when the exact time isn't important
  ✓ *Have you ever played at this festival?*
- we don't usually use **never** in questions
  ✓ *Have you ever played at this festival?*
  ✗ *Have you ~~never~~ played at this festival?*
- we use **never** to say 'not at any time'. It isn't used with **not/n't**.
  ✓ *He has never visited England.*
  ✗ *He ~~hasn't~~ never visited England.*
- we put **never** and **ever** between **have** and the past participle
  ✓ *I have never played in a group.*
  ✗ *I ~~never have~~ played in a group.*
  ✗ *Have ~~ever you~~ played in a group?*

2 Are the sentences correct? Correct the incorrect sentences.
1. I haven't never been to a festival.
   <u>I have never been to a festival.</u>
2. Have ever you sung in a choir or group?
   _____
3. She has never seen a living statue.
   _____
4. Has he never played in an orchestra?
   _____
5. They never have visited an art gallery.
   _____
6. He hasn't never met a famous person.
   _____

Collocations

Remember that:
- different verbs go with different nouns. Don't use the wrong verb!
  ✓ *Have you done your homework?*
  ✗ *Have you ~~made~~ your homework?*
  ✓ *I made a lot of mistakes in the exam.*
  ✗ *I ~~did~~ a lot of mistakes in the exam.*

3 Put the words and phrases in the correct place in the table.

~~a drawing~~   a presentation   photos   art   money
a work of art   graffiti   copies of something

Do	Make	Take
a drawing		

Spell it right! Past participles

Remember that:
- we form the present perfect with subject + have(n't)/has(n't) + past participle. We don't use the past simple.
- with irregular verbs, the past simple form of the verb and the past participle are often different. Look at the irregular verb table on page 126 of the Student's Book.
  ✓ *I have never taken a really cool photo.*
  ✓ *I have never ~~took~~ a really cool photo.*

4 Write the correct past simple and past participle form of the verbs.

Infinitive	Past simple	Past participle
take	took	taken
give		
speak		
do		
know		
sing		

4 Adventure

Vocabulary

Expressions with *go*

1 ★ Use the clues to complete the crossword.

4 across: s a i l i n g

Across
4 You need a boat and a good wind for this activity.
5 You can go on rides if you go here.
6 You can do this inside on a wall, or outside in the mountains.
7 You do this in snow in the mountains in winter.

Down
1 You do this kind of visit with another school.
2 Young people often stay in this place in the summer holidays.
3 You do this type of long walk in the mountains.
4 Going on one of these is a good way to see wild animals.
5 You do this with a guide who shows you a place and tells you about it.

2 ★ Match the verbs with the nouns in Exercise 1.
1 Things you go on: a ___safari___ , a school _____ , a guided _____
2 Activities with go: _____ , _____ , _____ , _____
3 A thing you go to: summer _____ , _____

3 ★★ Complete the email about Gemma's summer. Use the complete nouns from Exercise 2.

Hi Uncle Rob,
I have a problem this summer and I don't know what to do. All my friends are doing something exciting. Joe is going to a ¹ _theme park_ in California for a week. Maria is going to ² _____ in Wales to do rafting with her sister. She loves camping, and she's bought new mountain boots for when they go ³ _____ . It sounds fun! Alex is unhappy because his parents have decided to go to Greece. His mum wants to go on a ⁴ _____ of ancient ruins – boring! Emma has gone to Tanzania on a ⁵ _____ with her grandparents. Isn't that amazing? I wanted to visit my friend in Germany (do you remember she came here on a ⁶ _____ in May?), but she's gone rock ⁷ _____ in the Alps – too dangerous for me! Anyway, Mum and Dad want to go ⁸ _____ in Colorado (there's snow there in August!), but I want to go to the beach. Can I come and stay in Menorca with you and my cousins like last year? We could go ⁹ _____ in your little boat again. It would be fantastic.
What do you think?
Love,
Gemma

4 ★★★ What are your favourite holiday activities? Have you ever done any of the things in Exercise 1? Write at least five sentences. Use a dictionary if necessary.

I've never been on a cruise but I think it would be fun.

Unit 4 37

Language focus 1

Present perfect with *still*, *yet*, *already* and *just*

1 ★ **Complete the sentences with the present perfect and *just*. Use the verbs in brackets.**

1 'What's that CD?'
   'I *'ve just bought* it from a great busker in town.' (buy)
2 'What are those kids doing?' 'Juggling! They _____ how to do it!' (learn)
3 'Be careful! We _____ this door.' (paint)
4 'He looks tired.' 'Yes, he _____ a marathon!' (finish)
5 'What are you watching?' 'A film. I _____ it.' (download)
6 'Where did you put my book? I know you _____ it!' (move)

2 ★ **Circle the correct options.**

1 We haven't gone to the theme park **still** / **yet**. It's next week.
2 Nicky **still** / **already** hasn't packed for her school exchange visit tomorrow!
3 Have you put on suncream **yet** / **still** today?
4 We arrived on Saturday and I've **already** / **still** been sailing twice. It's great!
5 They've **already** / **yet** decided which mountain to climb, I think.
6 My grandparents **yet** / **still** haven't arrived home after their guided tour of Colombia.

3 ★★ **Put the words in the correct order to make sentences.**

1 your / been / yet / you / Have / exchange / on / school?
   Have you been on your school exchange yet?
2 Brigitte / arrived / already / has / my / at / house
   _____
3 climbing / started / I / haven't / the / still / course
   _____
4 yet / castle / haven't / the / seen / They
   _____
5 to / decided / She / hasn't / what / do / still
   _____
6 you / ruins / seen / Have / yet / the / ?
   _____
7 homework / our / haven't / still / We / done
   _____

4 ★★ **Complete the phone conversation. Use the verbs in the box and the adverbs in brackets.**

| visit Cambridge   be climbing |
| go   be̶   not tidy   not tell   start |

Mum: Are you enjoying the summer camp?
Craig: Yes, but it's going really quickly! We ¹*'ve already been* (already) here a week.
Mum: ² _____ (yet)?
Craig: Yes, I have – we've got a climbing wall here. And we ³ _____ (already) sailing twice, and trekking!
Mum: Great! What other plans have you got?
Craig: Well, we ⁴ _____ (yet). We're going on a guided tour of two university colleges, but the camp organiser ⁵ _____ (still) us which day. OK, Mum, I've got to go. We all help around the camp site. I ⁶ _____ (still) my things today! My group is cooking dinner and my friends ⁷ _____ (already) in the kitchen.

5 ★★★ **Imagine you are on a school exchange to London. Write sentences about things you have and haven't done. Use *still*, *yet*, *already* and *just* and the ideas in the box.**

| s̶e̶e̶ ̶B̶i̶g̶ ̶B̶e̶n̶   meet my new teacher |
| go out with my new friends   buy new clothes |
| speak a lot of English   go into the city centre |

1 *I haven't seen Big Ben yet.*
2 _____
3 _____
4 _____
5 _____
6 _____

38 Unit 4

Listening and vocabulary

Listening

1 ★ 🔊 04 **Listen to a family from London talking about their holiday. Which sentence is true?**
  a They are looking online at big hotels in lots of different countries.
  b They are looking on an international house exchange website to find another family to exchange houses with.
  c They find lots of holiday offers online but they all want to go to a different place.

2 ★★ 🔊 04 **Listen again. Who is it? Write M for Mum, D for Dad, L for Laura and K for Kevin.**
  1 _M_ has found lots of possible holiday places on a website.
  2 ___ wants to go somewhere new for a change.
  3 ___ suggests somewhere with water sports.
  4 ___ doesn't want to go to a place with nothing to do in the evenings.
  5 ___ likes an apartment in a city famous for art and culture.
  6 ___ notices another family don't want a holiday in London.
  7 ___ suggests going to another big city closer to London.
  8 ___ has a friend who's been there and liked it.
  9 ___ says he/she has wanted to go there for a long time.
  10 ___ thinks they should email the family in Amsterdam.

Phrasal verbs (1)

3 ★ **Match the words in bold with one of the phrasal verbs in the box.**

> chill out   ~~pick up~~   come back
> look around   set off   find out

  1 When my dad worked in Japan he tried to **learn** some Japanese from friends and neighbours.   _pick up_
  2 I love Saturday afternoons, when I can **relax** with my friends.   _____
  3 When we visit our village we always **start the journey** at six in the morning.   _____
  4 My granny loves going on guided tours so she can **discover** the history of a place.   _____
  5 After we arrived at the hotel, we went to **explore** the town.   _____
  6 I always like the day we **return** from our holidays, because I see my friends again.   _____

4 ★★ **Complete the text with the phrasal verbs from Exercise 3.**

BORED? NOTHING TO DO?

TRY OUR DAY TRIP TO BRIGHTON!

We ¹ _set off_ from Victoria Station at 9.30 and ² _____ at 8 o'clock in the evening. There's lots of time to ³ _____ Brighton's many boutique shops. You can ⁴ _____ more about historical Brighton by going on our optional guided tour of the city centre, or maybe you prefer to ⁵ _____ at the beach. Learning English? You can ⁶ _____ more English here than in a classroom!

DON'T MISS IT!

Language focus 2

Present perfect with *for* and *since*

1 ★ **Complete the sentences in the box.**

> We can use the present perfect with *for* or *since* to talk about an action that started in the ¹_____ and continues in the ²_____ .
> Use ³_____ with a period of time.
> Use ⁴_____ with a specific date or time.

2 ★★ Circle the correct options in the text.

We haven't had a holiday in the mountains since ¹(2010)/ three years. We had a tent then, but we've had this camper van since ² last year / a year. My parents have wanted to go to the Alps for ³ three years ago / a long time, so this year we're in Switzerland. We've been here for ⁴ yesterday / five days, and it's rained every day since ⁵ then / five days. It hasn't been this wet on holiday since ⁶ three years / the time we went to England!

3 ★★ **Write present perfect sentences with the prompts. Use *for* or *since*.**

1. My grandparents / live / their flat / forty years
   <u>My grandparents have lived in their flat for forty years.</u>
2. We / not go / on holiday / six months
   _____
3. My sister / work / in Geneva / 2009
   _____
4. They / not visit us / a long time
   _____
5. I / not see / her / 2012
   _____
6. He / want / to go to Brazil / last year
   _____

Present perfect and past simple

4 ★★ **Complete the conversation with the correct tense of the verbs in brackets.**

A: ¹ <u>Have you ever been</u> (you go) on a school exchange?
B: Yes, I have. Last year I ² _____ (go) to France.
A: Where ³ _____ (you go)?
B: Bordeaux. I ⁴ _____ (never see) such fantastic beaches.
A: What ⁵ _____ (you do) there?
B: We ⁶ _____ (go) sailing and surfing.
A: ⁷ _____ the French students _____ (come) here yet?
B: Yes, they're here now, in fact! They ⁸ _____ (be) here for a week.
A: So what ⁹ _____ (they do) so far?
B: Well, we ¹⁰ _____ (cook) them some traditional food, and they ¹¹ _____ (go) on a guided tour of the town.

5 ★★★ **Write a conversation about a trip. Use the one in Exercise 4 to help you. Use the present perfect and the past simple.**

A: Have you ever been to a summer camp?
B: Yes, I have. I went to one …

Explore interesting adjectives

6 ★★ **Complete the sentences with the adjectives in the box.**

> incredible   amazing   ~~spectacular~~
> important   perfect

1. The island has got high mountains and a volcano. The landscape is really <u>spectacular</u> !
2. The mountains are amazing and it's the _____ place for climbing.
3. The view from the sea on the boat is absolutely _____ .
4. An _____ part of learning how to ski is learning how to fall!
5. Going on safari was the most _____ experience I've ever had.

Reading

1 ★ **Read the text about two holidays. What have they got in common?**
a They are both trekking holidays for families with teenagers.
b On both trips you stay in luxury hotels.
c Both holidays include a four-day trek in the mountains.

Bored with your holidays?
Discover a new world with *Discovery*

Discovery has organised great holidays for 25 years, and we've just started holidays especially for families with teenagers. Our trips are carefully planned, and experienced, well-trained tour guides take groups of up to 15 people. **Porters** carry your **luggage**, so you can enjoy the **scenery**, and our cooks prepare delicious food every night.

Nepal Adventure Tour
Days 1–2 Chill out in Kathmandu, Nepal's capital city, where there are beautiful temples and monkeys climbing in the trees.
Days 3–10 The Annapurna Trek is spectacular, with amazing views of some of the world's highest mountains. We offer optional white-water rafting through the rapids. You sleep in **teahouses**, eat pancakes for breakfast and at dinner eat curry with your fingers, Nepalese style.
Days 11–12 The jungle of Chitwan National Park is a great place to relax after the trek. You can ride the elephants, and look for rare one-horned rhinos.
Days 13–14 Back to Kathmandu to shop for **souvenirs** in the bazaars.

Inca Trail For Teens
Days 1–3 Set off for Cusco, the ancient Inca capital. You can explore fascinating Inca ruins and look around this beautiful Spanish-style city. We also visit the colourful indigenous Pisac Market.
Day 4–5 We visit Misminay, where our Inca Trail porters live, to experience the traditional way of life of an Andean mountain village.
Days 6–7 Enjoy the **thrill** of white-water rafting or downhill mountain biking in the beautiful Sacred Valley.
Day 8–11 A four-day trek along the Inca Trail through spectacular scenery.
Day 12 Arrive at Machu Picchu and discover this ancient Inca citadel.
Days 13–14 Back to Cusco. Finish your holiday here shopping for souvenirs and chilling out.

2 ★★ **Complete the sentences with the words in *bold* from the text.**
1 I like travelling by train and looking out of the window at the _____ .
2 When I go on holiday, I always buy _____ to remind me of the places I've visited.
3 There's nothing like the _____ of a big rollercoaster – they are so exciting I always scream!
4 How much _____ have you got? You can only take 20 kilos on the plane.
5 In India the _____ are really hotel-restaurants, not cafés where you have a cup of tea.
6 The hotel _____ who carried our bags recommended a good restaurant.

3 ★★ **Read the text again. Circle the correct options.**
1 These holidays are especially for families with small children / **teenagers**.
2 There **is** / **isn't** an experienced person leading the group on both holidays.
3 There are views of **high mountains** / **ancient cities** in Nepal.
4 You **see** / **don't see** wild animals on the Inca Trail.
5 You can go cycling **in Nepal** / **on the Inca Trail**.
6 You visit temples in **Kathmandu** / **Cusco**.
7 You can go shopping at the **beginning** / **end** of both trips.
8 You see where the porters live in **Chitwan National Park** / **Misminay**.

4 ★★★ **Read the sentences from postcards. Are they from Nepal or the Inca Trail? Write N or I.**
1 We're going to spend a few days chilling out in Cusco. Do you want anything? *I*
2 Today we had a look around some ruins and went to a market. ___
3 I've never ridden an elephant but it's a great way to see the jungle. ___
4 We've been here for two days and we've seen some amazing temples. ___
5 We went so fast on the bikes that I didn't have time to look at the scenery! ___
6 The curries are delicious but I don't like eating with my fingers! ___

5 ★★★ **Do you like this kind of holiday? Which of the two do you prefer and why? Write four or five sentences.**

Writing

A travel blog

1 Read Andy's travel blog. What kind of holiday is a *cruise*?

My holiday blog
a Mediterranean cruise

We've been here for six days and what ¹ _an amazing ship_ ! Since we left Barcelona, I've been on the climbing wall and played volleyball and mini-golf. There's also the 'Ocean Adventure Teen Club', with its own swimming pool and activities. What ² _____ to make friends! I'd like to stay on the ship all the time, but my parents insist I see everywhere we visit.

We've already stopped in Nice, Florence and Rome (what ³ _____ they have in Italy!), and Athens – hot, crowded, and what ⁴ _____ . We visited the island of Santorini yesterday, definitely my favourite place – what ⁵ _____ ! And we've just arrived at Mykonos. What ⁶ _____ they're having – I can hear the music from here!

More soon …
Andy

Our ship – Voyager of the Seas

The Gang

2 Read the blog again. Complete the text with the words in the box.

> an incredible party   an amazing ship
> delicious ice creams   boring ruins
> beautiful beaches   a fantastic way

3 Read the blog again and answer the questions.
1 What kind of holiday is Andy having?
   He's having a cruise.
2 Where did it start?
   _____
3 What activities has he done on the ship?
   _____
4 What do his parents make him do?
   _____
5 How many places has he seen?
   _____
6 What did he like about Italy?
   _____
7 Why didn't he like Athens?
   _____
8 Which place does he like best so far?
   _____

4 Read the blog again. Tick (✓) the things in the list that Andy writes about.

where you started ☐
where you've been ☐
how long you've been on the trip ☐
what you've eaten ☐
what you've done ☐
what you've seen ☐
your favourite place ☐
your favourite activities ☐
how you feel about something ☐

Useful language   Expressing how you feel, good or bad.

5 Complete the table with the adjectives in the box.

> awful   ~~incredible~~   amazing   disappointing
> boring   fantastic   ugly   spectacular   terrible

Good ☺	Bad ☹
incredible	

42   Unit 4

Writing

6 Read the sentences and write how you felt. Use the words in Exercise 5 to help you.

1 The Eiffel Tower was as good as we thought it would be.
   I thought it was fantastic.
2 I didn't think Hamburg was beautiful at all.
   _____
3 I almost fell asleep in the museum.
   _____
4 The food at the restaurant was disgusting.
   _____
5 There were tall mountains and beautiful lakes.
   _____
6 I couldn't believe it when I saw the tall buildings.
   _____

> **WRITING TIP**
> Make it better! ✓ ✓ ✓
> Use *What a/an* before singular countable nouns.
> Use *What* before singular uncountable and plural nouns.

7 Rewrite the sentences with *What* or *What a/an*.

1 It was a very exciting theme park.
   What an exciting theme park.
2 The fireworks were really spectacular.
   _____
3 The guided tour was very boring.
   _____
4 The landscape was incredible.
   _____
5 The souvenir shops were terrible.
   _____

8 Rewrite the sentences. Put the word in brackets in the correct place.

1 We've seen about 20 temples. (already)
   We've already seen about 20 temples.
2 I can't believe it was such a beautiful place. (still)
   _____
3 We haven't visited the museum. (yet)
   _____
4 They've gone skiing in the mountains. (just)
   _____

> **WRITING TIP**
> Make it better! ✓ ✓ ✓
> Use different ways to say 'my favourite …'.

9 Read the sentences. Which one does <u>not</u> mean *my favourite*?

1 The safari has been the best thing *so far*.
2 *I've never eaten a better* ice cream.
3 The guided tour was *quite good*.
4 There is *no better way* to spend a summer.
5 *By far* the best activity has been the climbing.

10 Read the blog again. Number the things in the list in the order they appear.

Andy's favourite place ___
how long Andy has been on the trip   1
what Andy has done ___
where Andy has been ___
where the trip started ___
how Andy feels about something ___

PLAN

11 Imagine you are on a cruise. Use the list in Exercise 10 and your imagination to make notes.

WRITE

12 Write a travel blog post about your trip. Look at page 49 of the Student's Book to help you.

_____
_____
_____
_____
_____
_____
_____
_____
_____
_____
_____
_____
_____
_____

CHECK

13 Check your writing. Can you say YES to these questions?

- Have you expressed how you feel – good and bad?
- Have you used sentences with *What a/an*?
- Are words like *still*, *already*, *yet* and *just* in the right place in the sentences?
- Have you used different ways to say *my favourite*?
- Are the spelling and punctuation correct?

Do you need to write a second draft?

4 Review

Vocabulary
Expressions with *go*

1 Match the trips with the places and things.

1 go climbing — *d*
2 go on a safari — __
3 go skiing — __
4 go to a theme park — __
5 go on a guided tour — __
6 go to summer camp — __
7 go on a school exchange — __

a activities for young people
b historic buildings and museums
c roller coasters, rides, restaurants
d mountains
e a school in another country
f mountains and snow
g wild animals

Total: 6

Phrasal verbs (1)

2 Use a word from each box to make phrasal verbs and complete the postcard.

| find chill pick come ~~look~~ set |

| out (x2) up ~~around~~ back off |

Dear Lou,

We've had a fantastic time here in Berlin. We've had plenty of time to ¹ *look around* the city. It was fun to ² _____ about the city's history and culture, and we also managed to ³ _____ some German! There are a lot of cafés to eat ice cream and ⁴ _____. Tonight we have to go to bed early because we have to ⁵ _____ at 6 am tomorrow morning. Our holiday is over and it's time to ⁶ _____ home!

Annie

Total: 5

Language focus
Present perfect with *still, yet, already* and *just*

3 Circle the correct options to complete each mini-conversation.

1 A: Has your sister left for London **yet** / **still**?
   B: Yes, she left yesterday but she **already** / **still** hasn't phoned us.
2 A: Have you booked your hotel **still** / **yet**?
   B: No, I **already** / **still** haven't decided which one I prefer.
3 A: Have you seen Buckingham Palace **still** / **yet**?
   B: No, but we've **still** / **already** seen some great museums and art galleries.
4 A: Why is your hair wet?
   B: I've **just** / **still** come back from swimming.

Total: 6

Present perfect with *for* and *since*

4 Circle the correct options.

1 I've lived here **for** / **since** January.
2 Suzanne has played the guitar **for** / **since** a very long time.
3 We've been friends **for** / **since** we were little children.
4 I haven't seen you **for** / **since** ages.
5 Mark has had his car **for** / **since** five years.
6 They haven't visited us **for** / **since** last year.

Total: 5

Present perfect and past simple

5 Complete the mini-conversations with the correct tense of the verbs in brackets.

1 A: *Have you ever been* (you ever go) to Italy?
   B: Yes, we _____ (go) there last summer.
2 A: I _____ (eat) some octopus yesterday.
   B: Really? I _____ (never eat) octopus.
3 A: _____ (you see) this film?
   B: Yes, I _____ (see) it twice.

Total: 5

44 Unit 4 Review

Language builder

6 Complete the email with the missing words. Circle the correct options.

1	a ever	b never	c yet
2	a always go	b always are going	c go always
3	a go	b 've been	c went
4	a were taking	b 've taken	c take
5	a comes	b came	c was coming
6	a don't take usually	b usually don't take	c don't usually take
7	a take	b 'm taking	c was taking
8	a should	b have	c shouldn't
9	a have	b 've to	c should
10	a you doing	b you are doing	c are you doing
11	a You have to	b You do have to	c Do you have to

☐ Total: 10

Your MAIL (+) New Reply | ▼

Hi Bruno,

This is the first day of our trip to Switzerland. I've ¹___ been to Switzerland before. The mountains are really amazing! I'm here with my parents and my best friend, Susan. We ²___ on holiday together every year. Yesterday, we ³___ hiking in the forest. When we ⁴___ pictures of some flowers, a small goat ⁵___ up to us and started eating them! I ⁶___ a lot of photos, but this year I ⁷___ a lot because I want to make a photo blog when I get back home. I ⁸___ stop writing now because I ⁹___ to get up early tomorrow. What ¹⁰___ this summer? ¹¹___ do any schoolwork?

Write soon,

Janey

Vocabulary builder

7 Circle the correct options.

1 Going on a ___ is a great way to meet students from other countries.
   a safari   b school exchange   c guided tour
2 While I was in Poland I ___ a few words of Polish.
   a set up   b showed up   c picked up
3 It was boiling for about three days and then the ___ went away.
   a snowstorm   b heat wave   c lightning
4 We looked at the ___ but we didn't know where we were.
   a map   b compass   c torch
5 Sarah hasn't ___ the photos online yet.
   a hung   b given   c posted
6 I haven't had much time ___ myself yet. I've been very busy.
   a on   b by   c with
7 Can you set ___ the drums before we start playing?
   a on   b down   c up
8 We went on a ___ tour of the castle and gardens.
   a guiding   b guided   c guide
9 You have to blow very hard to make a sound on the ___ .
   a trumpet   b piano   c banjo
10 I'm hungry because I haven't even ___ a snack today.
   a had   b taken   c done

☐ Total: 9

Speaking

8 Put the words in the correct order to make questions for signing up for an activity.

1 about / What / then / food, / ?
   What about food, then?
2 trip / long / How / is / the / ?
   _____
3 include / the price / Does / food / ?
   _____
4 bring / need / I / do / What / to / ?
   _____
5 a few / Can / about / I / you / the trip things / ask / ?
   _____
6 only / it / for / experienced / climbers / Is / ?
   _____

☐ Total: 5

☐ Total: 51

Unit 4 Review 45

Get it right! Unit 4

Present perfect with *still*, *yet*, *already* and *just*

Remember that:
- we put *still* directly after the subject
  ✓ I still haven't adjusted to life at sea.
  ✗ I haven't adjusted to life at sea still.
- we put *yet* after the complete verb phrase
  ✓ Have you brushed your teeth yet?
  ✗ Have you brushed yet your teeth?
- we normally put *just* and *already* between *have* and the past participle
  ✓ I've already packed my swimming costume.
  ✗ I've packed already my swimming costume.
  ✓ I have just climbed up and down the mast.
  ✗ I just have climbed up and down the mast.

1 Are the sentences correct? Correct the incorrect sentences.

1 I just have returned from my climbing trip.
   I have just returned from my climbing trip.

2 I haven't still tried skiing, but I'm sure I'll enjoy it.
   _____

3 I haven't been yet there, but I really want to go.
   _____

4 She has made already a lot of friends on the adventure holiday.
   _____

5 They just have bought tickets for a guided tour of the city.
   _____

6 My sister is five, so she yet hasn't been sailing.
   _____

7 I have just received a letter from my grandfather.
   _____

8 He said he would call me, but I still haven't heard from him.
   _____

Present perfect with *for* and *since*

Remember that:
- we use *for* with periods of time
  ✓ We've been on the road in our camper van for ten days.
  ✗ We've been on the road in our camper van since ten days.
- we use *since* with a specific date, time or event
  ✓ We haven't had anything to eat since lunchtime.
  ✗ We haven't had anything to eat for lunchtime.

2 Circle the correct words.

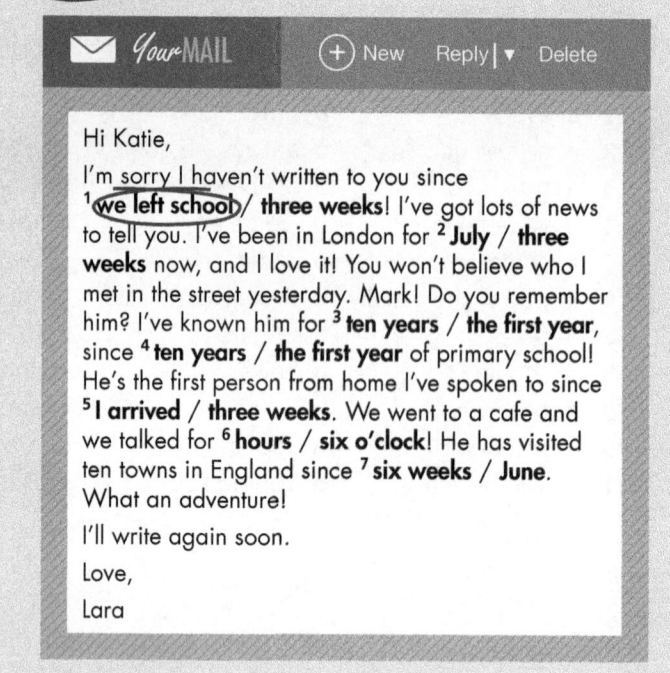

✉ Your MAIL   (+) New   Reply|▼   Delete

Hi Katie,
I'm sorry I haven't written to you since ¹**we left school**/ three weeks! I've got lots of news to tell you. I've been in London for ² **July** / **three weeks** now, and I love it! You won't believe who I met in the street yesterday. Mark! Do you remember him? I've known him for ³ **ten years** / **the first year**, since ⁴ **ten years** / **the first year** of primary school! He's the first person from home I've spoken to since ⁵ **I arrived** / **three weeks**. We went to a cafe and we talked for ⁶ **hours** / **six o'clock**! He has visited ten towns in England since ⁷ **six weeks** / **June**. What an adventure!
I'll write again soon.
Love,
Lara

Expressions with *go*

Remember that:
- we use *go* + *-ing* to talk about doing an activity. We never use a preposition between *go* and the activity.
  ✓ Did you go climbing?
  ✗ Did you go for climbing?
  ✗ Did you go to climbing?

3 Find and correct four more mistakes with *go* in the poster.

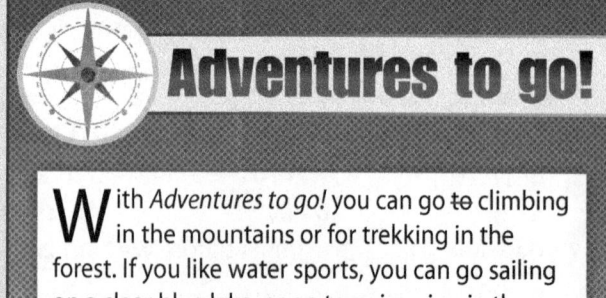

Adventures to go!

With *Adventures to go!* you can go ~~to~~ climbing in the mountains or for trekking in the forest. If you like water sports, you can go sailing on a clear blue lake, or go to swimming in the sea. Why not go to camping for a few days? Or, if you like, you can go to a hotel instead. If you're feeling tired from all these activities, you can go on a guided bus tour or go to a safari park for the day. And there's even a bus to the city every day for those who want to go to shopping. The fun never stops with *Adventures to go!*

www.adventures2go.net

Speaking extra

Giving your opinion

1 ★ ▶ 1.3 Put the words in order to make sentences from the Real talk video in the Student's Book.
1 cities / I / great / indoor / think / for / are / activities
_____
2 your / small / Everyone / town / knows / in / problems / a
_____
3 lot / in / country / a / There / shops / aren't / and concerts / of / the
_____
4 air / unhealthy / The / is / city / in / dirty and / the
_____
5 different / a / neighbourhood / You / go / park or / can / to / every day
_____

2 ★★ 🔊 09 Listen and choose the correct answer.
Conversation 1:
1 The boy and girl live in the **city** / **country**.
Conversation 2:
2 The boy thinks he **has got** / **hasn't got** lots of friends.
3 The girl **agrees** / **doesn't agree**.
Conversation 3:
4 The girl goes to a **big** / **small** school.
5 Everybody laughed at him because he broke his **school bag** / **glasses**.

3 ★ Read the conversation. Where does Amy want to live?

Amy:	I hate winter! It's freezing and there's another snow storm tomorrow.
Jamie:	Yes, but at least our PE class will be indoors today.
Amy:	I suppose ¹_____ . But it's so boring. We can't go anywhere.
Jamie:	Maybe, ²_____ where would you like to go?
Amy:	To the beach. I ³_____ life in California would be better. Why can't I live there? It'd be great to live in California.
Jamie:	I don't ⁴_____ . I like winter here. There's lots of snow and we can go skiing every day. It's great!
Amy:	Well, I ⁵_____ think so. You know I hate skiing. I'd prefer to be warm all the time, with sunny weather! Like in California.
Jamie:	Perhaps ⁶_____ right. But you'd have to put on sun cream all the time, carry a water bottle and wear sunglasses.
Amy:	Yes! Great!

4 ★★ 🔊 10 Complete the conversation in Exercise 3 with the words in the box. Then listen and check.

don't   so   you're   but   agree   reckon

Pronunciation focus: Agreeing and disagreeing

5 ★ 🔊 11 Where does the voice go up in these sentences? Listen and repeat.
1 I think living in a warm country would be great.
2 I don't think I'd like to live in a cold country.
3 I reckon a big school is better.
4 I don't agree.
5 I think life would be great.

6 ★ 🔊 12 Listen to the conversation. What does Eva think is a good way to see the countryside?

7 ★★★ 🔊 12 Listen again and complete the conversation.

Nathan:	I love going camping. ¹_____ it's great to sleep in a sleeping bag under the stars.
Eva:	Camping? No, thanks. ²_____ sleeping under the stars is great at all. You're probably freezing and in this country there's always heavy rain.
Nathan:	That's ³_____ . But where's your sense of adventure?
Eva:	⁴_____ you have to be mad to go camping.
Nathan:	⁵_____ it's the best way to see the countryside and to get some fresh air.
Eva:	⁶_____ . There are lots of ways to do that. You can go cycling or trekking. That's what I like doing.
Nathan:	Yes, ⁷_____ . But when you go camping, you have more time and it's more relaxing.
Eva:	Fine, but I still prefer to sleep in a big comfortable bed in a hotel.

8 ★★ 🔊 12 Listen again and check your answers. Then listen and repeat the conversation.

Speaking extra

Offering to help

1 ⭐ ▶ **2.3** Match the sentence halves from the Real talk video in the Student's Book.
1 It was an enormous job ___
2 A good friend doesn't have to do anything, ___
3 I'm not sad very often but when I am ___
4 I can't always talk to my parents. ___
5 Sometimes it's hard ___

a I only want to talk to my friend.
b It's easier to talk to my friend.
c but a real friend never lies to you.
d but fun doing it all together.
e they just have to be there.

2 ⭐⭐ 🔊 **13** Listen and choose the correct answer.

Conversation 1:
1 The girl is sending a message to say **hello / sorry**.

Conversation 2:
2 The girl is doing a **Maths / English** problem.
3 In the end she **understands / doesn't understand**.

Conversation 3:
4 The boy is doing a **History / Art** project.
5 He needs a photo of a **ship / computer**.

3 ⭐ Read the conversation. Where do Lily and Chloe look for information first?

Lily:	Hey, Chloe. Can I ¹_____ you something?
Chloe:	Yeah, sure. What's up?
Lily:	It's this Social Science project. I have to write a biography of Nelson Mandela, but I'm not ²_____ where to start.
Chloe:	He was very famous. What do you ³_____ ?
Lily:	Well, where do I find out about him?
Chloe:	I think you should look on the Internet first. Here, ⁴_____ me help you.
Lily:	Thanks. That's really nice of you!
Chloe:	It's easy. ⁵_____ you have to do is look at an online encyclopaedia. Read about him and make notes of the most important moments in his life.
Lily:	I'm not very good at deciding what's important.
Chloe:	Don't worry. I'll give you a ⁶_____ if you like.
Lily:	Great! That's really kind.

4 ⭐⭐ 🔊 **14** Complete the conversation in Exercise 3 with the words in the box. Then listen and check.

> hand   sure   need   All   ask   let

Pronunciation focus: Linking words

5 ⭐ 🔊 **15** Listen to the sentences. Which words are linked? Listen and repeat.
1 Can I ask you something?
2 I'll give you a hand.
3 Let me show you.
4 I'm not sure how to do it.
5 What do you need?

6 ⭐ 🔊 **16** Listen to the conversation. What two things does Lewis want to know?

7 ⭐⭐⭐ 🔊 **16** Listen again and complete the conversation.

Oliver:	Hi Lewis? What are you doing?
Lewis:	Oh, hi Oliver. Just some homework. But I'm so tired.
Oliver:	Here, ¹_____ if you like.
Lewis:	Thanks. I'm not very good at History.
Oliver:	It's not that difficult. ²_____ is write the correct date.
Lewis:	Yes, but I'm not very good at remembering dates. Especially when I'm tired!
Oliver:	Yeah, I know. You forgot my birthday! ³_____ ?
Lewis:	Let's see. When did the Romans come to Britain?
Oliver:	That's in Chapter 1 of the History book. ⁴_____ .
Lewis:	Thanks. Oliver, ⁵_____ something?
Oliver:	Sure. What's up?
Lewis:	How do I get a good night's sleep?
Oliver:	You have to feel relaxed before you go to sleep.
Lewis:	OK, but ⁶_____ do that.
Oliver:	Well let's finish this History quiz first. Let's see … the Romans in Britain … Lewis? … Lewis?

8 ⭐⭐ 🔊 **16** Listen again and check your answers. Then listen and repeat the conversation.

Speaking extra

Invitations and arrangements

1 ★ ▶ 3.3 **Complete the sentences from the Real talk video in the Student's Book with the words in the box.**

birthday   years   crowd   cheaper   people

1 I love being part of a _____ .
2 I don't like listening to music with a lot of _____ around.
3 I went to my first one when I was only five _____ old.
4 I saw One Direction for my _____ last year and they were amazing.
5 Cinema tickets are _____ than concert tickets.

2 ★★ 🔊 17 **Listen and write the answers.**

Conversation 1:
1 What's the photo exhibition about?
_____

Conversation 2:
2 What are the girls talking about?
_____
3 Where are they going to meet?
_____

Conversation 3:
4 What kind of festival is it?
_____
5 How are the boys going to get there?
_____

3 ★ **Read the conversation. When are Will and Carol going to buy concert tickets?**

Will:	Oh, look, The King Birds are coming to do a concert.
Carol:	Great! Do you ¹_____ going to see them?
Will:	Yeah, why not? ²_____ I ask my dad to get tickets?
Carol:	No, let's go and buy them ³_____ .
Will:	⁴_____ good.
Carol:	Where are they selling them?
Will:	In *Piano Sounds* – that shop in town.
Carol:	How ⁵_____ going this afternoon?
Will:	OK, what time shall we meet?
Carol:	After school?
Will:	That's a great ⁶_____ ! See you later.

4 ★★ 🔊 18 **Complete the conversation in Exercise 3 with the words in the box. Then listen and check your answers.**

about   Shall   together   Sounds   idea   fancy

Pronunciation focus: Invitations

5 ★ 🔊 19 **Listen to the invitations. Does the voice go up or down? Listen and repeat.**
1 Do you fancy going to a concert?
2 Shall I ask Rebecca to come with us?
3 How about going after school?
4 Shall I go to your house?
5 How about going for an ice cream later?

6 ★ 🔊 20 **Listen to the conversation. Where are Liam and Connor going to practise?**

7 ★★★ 🔊 20 **Listen again and complete the conversation.**

Connor:	Hey, Liam, you play the guitar, don't you?
Liam:	Yes, I do.
Connor:	Well, I play the drums. ¹_____ playing together?
Liam:	Yeah, ²_____ ? Can we practise at your house?
Connor:	I think so. I'll have to check with my parents.
Liam:	³_____ Helen to come, too? She plays the piano and her friend Florence plays the bass guitar.
Connor:	That's ⁴_____ ! We can all practise together.
Liam:	Hey, ⁵_____ starting a band?
Connor:	Well, let's practise together first.
Liam:	What time shall ⁶_____ ?
Connor:	I'll talk to my parents and then I'll send you a message.
Liam:	⁷_____ ! I'll start thinking of a band name. Liam and Friends? One Liam? Liam and the Gang? …

8 ★★ 🔊 20 **Listen again and check your answers. Then listen and repeat the conversation.**

Speaking extra

Signing up for an activity

1 ★ ▶ 4.3 Complete the sentences from the Real talk video in the Student's Book with the words in the box.

| nervous times scary awesome cold |

1 It was really good fun but _____ at the same time.
2 It was so loud and really _____ . It was July so I didn't expect that.
3 I was always too scared but last year I jumped. It was _____ .
4 I was really _____ before I started.
5 I've been on the biggest roller coaster in the world five _____ .

2 ★★ 🔊 21 Listen and choose the correct words.

Conversation 1:
1 The boy is going to do a **skiing / sailing** course.
Conversation 2:
2 The girl is going **climbing / trekking**.
3 The boy should wear **sun cream / sunglasses**.
Conversation 3:
4 The girl is going **climbing / whitewater rafting**.
5 They're going to go **on foot / by bus**.

3 ★ Read the conversation. How long will Justin be at the theme park?

Justin: Can I ¹_____ you a few things about the trip to the theme park?
Guide: Sure. What ²_____ you like to know?
Justin: First of all, what time are we leaving tomorrow?
Guide: The bus leaves at 10 o'clock in the morning and you'll be back here at about five o'clock.
Justin: So how ³_____ is the journey to the theme park?
Guide: It's not far, about 40 minutes.
Justin: OK, what do we need to ⁴_____ ?
Guide: Nothing really. Maybe some money for water or sweets, but lunch is included.
Justin: Does the price ⁵_____ all the different rides?
Guide: Yes, you can go on everything.
Justin: Even the *Monster Mountain* roller coaster?
Guide: Everything.
Justin: OK, where can I ⁶_____ up?
Guide: Right here. What's your name? …

4 ★★ 🔊 22 Complete the conversation in Exercise 3 with the words in the box. Then listen and check.

| include long would sign bring ask |

Pronunciation focus: Asking for information

5 ★ 🔊 23 Listen to the questions. Does the voice go up or down? Listen and repeat.
1 Where can I sign up?
2 What about food?
3 Can I ask you a few things about the course?
4 Does the price include transport?
5 How long is the trip?
6 What do I need to bring?

6 ★ 🔊 24 Listen to the conversation. Why is Taylor surprised?

7 ★★★ 🔊 24 Listen again and complete the conversation.

Jacob: Hi, Taylor. Are you going on the sailing trip tomorrow?
Taylor: Yeah. I can't wait. This is my third time! Are you going too?
Jacob: I don't know. I've never been sailing. ¹_____ a few things about the trip?
Taylor: Sure.
Jacob: ²_____ ? I mean how long are we out in the boats?
Taylor: Oh, we're usually out for about three or four hours.
Jacob: OK, wow! That's a long time … and ³_____ ?
Taylor: Well, swim shorts, shoes that you can get wet … and that's all I think.
Jacob: ⁴_____ life jackets?
Taylor: Oh, no. You'll get one of those.
Jacob: And ⁵_____ some swimming lessons first?
Taylor: Swimming lessons? Err …no. You can't swim?
Jacob: Well, no.

8 ★★ 🔊 24 Listen again and check your answers. Then listen and repeat the conversation.

Language focus extra

Wh- questions

1 Complete the mini-conversations with the words in the box.

> Where ~~How old~~ Whose
> How When What Who

1. A: ____How old____ is your dad?
   B: He's thirty-nine.
2. A: _____ do you walk to school with?
   B: My sister.
3. A: _____ did you have lunch yesterday?
   B: In the school café.
4. A: _____ bicycle is that?
   B: I think it's Sara's.
5. A: _____ are you?
   B: Fine, thanks.
6. A: _____ is the first thing you do when you get up?
   B: I have a shower.
7. A: _____ do you usually do your homework?
   B: In the morning before school!

Adjectives and adverbs

2 Complete the sentences with the correct form of the adjective or adverb.

1. *careful*
   A: Please be ____careful____ when you ride to school.
   B: Don't worry. I always ride ____carefully____ .
2. *quick*
   A: We need to walk more _____ or we'll be late.
   B: I'm sorry, I'm not a _____ walker.
3. *easy*
   A: That was an _____ test, wasn't it?
   B: Yes, I think everyone passed it _____ .
4. *good*
   A: Sam sings really _____ doesn't she?
   B: Yes, she's a really _____ singer.

Comparative and superlative adjectives

3 Circle the correct options.

1. My sister is **older** / **the oldest** than me.
2. Driving is **dangerouser** / **more dangerous** than flying.
3. This is the **worse** / **worst** holiday of my life!
4. I've got long hair, but Anna's hair is **more long** / **longer** .
5. You are the **more** / **most** intelligent person in the class.
6. It's the **most funny** / **funniest** film that I've got on DVD.

Comparative and superlative adverbs

4 Rewrite the sentences. Use a comparative or superlative adverb.

1. Dan is a slower runner than me.
   Dan runs *more slowly than me* .
2. You are a better dancer than Jill.
   You dance _____ .
3. Bella is a more careful writer than the other students.
   Bella writes _____ .
4. I'm a quieter speaker than most people.
   I speak _____ .
5. Tom is the most dangerous driver in my family.
   Tom drives _____ .
6. You are the quickest reader.
   You read _____ .

Past simple

5 Complete the text with the past simple form of the verbs in brackets.

Last Saturday I ¹____was____ (be) at my friend Susan's thirteenth birthday. She ²_____ (have) a party at her house, and lots of people ³_____ (come). It ⁴_____ (start) at 8pm. I ⁵_____ (see) some friends there and we ⁶_____ (talk) and ⁷_____ (laugh) for hours. We also ⁸_____ (dance) and ⁹_____ (eat) lots of cake. I ¹⁰_____ (not want) the party to end!

6 Put the words in the correct order.

1. an / breakfast / ate / I / ago / hour
   I ate breakfast an hour ago.
2. week / last / party / had /a / Julia
   _____
3. do / last / did / night / What / you?
   _____
4. ill / felt / morning / I / yesterday
   _____
5. me / call / you / night / didn't / last / Why?
   _____
6. ago / I / film / this / saw / months / three
   _____

Language focus extra

Present simple and continuous

1 Circle the correct options.
1 I don't want to go outside. It **rains** / **'s raining**.
2 **Do you walk** / **Are you walking** to school every day?
3 I usually **eat** / **am eating** some fruit after lunch.
4 **Do you watch** / **Are you watching** the football match? It's really boring.
5 Emily can't come with us. She **does** / **'s doing** her homework.
6 I **don't usually go** / **'m not usually going** to bed until 11 o'clock.
7 Look! The baby **dances** / **is dancing**. Take a photo.
8 We **don't go** / **'re not going** shopping now. There's a snowstorm outside!

2 Complete the conversation. Use the present simple or the present continuous form of the verbs in brackets.

> **John:** Hello. ¹ _Are you doing_ (you do) anything special at the moment?
> **Katie:** Right now, I ² _____ (look after) my little brother. Why?
> **John:** What time ³ _____ (your mum get) home from work?
> **Katie:** She ⁴ _____ (work) late every Thursday, so at about half past eight. Why?
> **John:** They ⁵ _____ (show) the new Miley Cyrus film at the cinema on Main Street. My sister and I ⁶ _____ (think) about going. ⁷ _____ (you want) to come with us?
> **Katie:** Yes, please! Let's meet at the cinema at quarter to nine!
> **John:** Great. It ⁸ _____ (rain) so take an umbrella.

Past simple and past continuous

3 Circle the correct options.
1 I didn't hear that the teacher **talked** / **was talking** to me.
2 Dan **was sending** / **sent** me a text when I was playing tennis.
3 On holiday, we **went** / **were going** swimming every day.
4 We **were listening** / **listened** to loud music, but my dad told us to turn it down.
5 My mum **made** / **was making** lunch when I got home.
6 When I was young, we **were visiting** / **visited** my grandparents every weekend.
7 I **washed** / **was washing** my dad's car when it started to rain.
8 **Did you watch** / **Were you watching** the end of the film last night? What happened?
9 When you called Eva, she **played** / **was playing** the guitar.
10 After the basketball match, I **had** / **was having** a shower and went home.

4 Complete the sentences. Use the past simple or past continuous form of the verbs in brackets.

a When I ¹ _arrived_ (arrive) home after school yesterday, my family was very busy! My mum ² _____ (work), my brother ³ _____ (do) his homework and my sister ⁴ _____ (practise) the piano.

b Yesterday I ⁵ _____ (have) a shower when suddenly, I ⁶ _____ (hear) a strange noise coming from downstairs. I ⁷ _____ (get) out of the shower, ⁸ _____ (go) downstairs and then I ⁹ _____ (see) my cat with a mouse in his mouth!

5 Complete the text. Use the past simple or the past continuous form of the verbs in brackets.

When I woke up, it ¹ _was raining_ (rain). I ² _____ (walk) to the bathroom, but my brother ³ _____ (have) a shower. I ⁴ _____ (tell) him to be quick, and then I ⁵ _____ (go) to the kitchen. Dad ⁶ _____ (read) the newspaper, and Mum ⁷ _____ (listen) to the radio.
'⁸ _____ (you sleep) well?' asked Dad.
'No,' I said, 'I ⁹ _____ (have) a very strange dream about my English class. I ¹⁰ _____ (sit) at my desk when the teacher ¹¹ _____ (ask) me a question.'
'That's not very strange,' my mum said.
'Yes, but when I ¹² _____ (answer) the question, I ¹³ _____ (speak) really quietly and the teacher ¹⁴ _____ (not hear) me. Everyone ¹⁵ _____ (laugh) and then I ¹⁶ _____ (wake up)!'

Language focus extra

should

1 Two friends are planning a party. Write sentences and questions with *should*. Add extra words if necessary.

1. we / ask your parents for permission?
   '*Should we ask your parents for permission?*'
   'I asked them yesterday.'
2. we / invite?
   '_____,'
   'Everyone in the class.'
3. they / bring some food and drink?
   '_____,'
   'No, my mum is going to get everything.'
4. everyone / arrive / 8 pm. Is that OK?
   '_____,'
   'Yes, about 8 pm is fine.'
5. I / wear?
   '_____,'
   'Your blue skirt and white T-shirt.'
6. I / bring some dance music. What do you think?
   '_____,'
   'Yes, that's a good idea.'

must

2 Complete the sentences with *must* or *mustn't*.

1. You ___*mustn't*___ forget to call me tonight.
2. Students _____ write in pen, not pencil.
3. You _____ tell anyone. It's a secret.
4. Tell them that they _____ relax more. It's OK.
5. We _____ make a lot of noise. This is the library.
6. I _____ be late, because Dad gets angry.

3 Circle the correct options.

1. You **shouldn't** / must be scared to follow your dreams.
2. You **should** / **shouldn't** make promises you can't keep.
3. You're always tired. You really **should** / **mustn't** get more sleep.
4. You **must** / **should** listen more, and speak less.
5. You **must** / **mustn't** criticise other people. It's not nice.
6. You **must** / **shouldn't** wear your glasses. You can't see without them!
7. You **shouldn't** / **must** give up. Try again!
8. You **mustn't** / **shouldn't** drink that water. It'll make you sick.
9. You **must** / **should** do something creative if you're bored.

have to / don't have to

4 Complete the sentences and questions with the correct form of *have to*.

1. You ___*don't have to*___ phone. You can email for information.
2. At my school, we _____ play hockey, but there is a school team.
3. Doctors _____ study for seven or eight years.
4. Why _____ (she) do the exam again?
5. My brother _____ study much. He's really clever.
6. _____ (we) take a sleeping bag with us?
7. I _____ help around the house but I don't mind.
8. It's OK. You _____ speak quietly. The baby woke up a few minutes ago.

5 Complete the sentences with *don't have to* or *mustn't* and the verbs in the box.

> have go ~~use~~ do play
> speak forget watch

1. You ___*mustn't use*___ your mobile phone. It's not allowed.
2. You _____ your homework now. You can do it later.
3. We _____ a film. We can go out if you like.
4. You _____ your first aid kit when you go camping.
5. You _____ a snack now. We're going to have dinner in 10 minutes.
6. We _____ to school today. It's a holiday.
7. It's OK. You _____ slowly. I understand you.
8. It's 1 o'clock in the morning. You _____ your guitar now. Go to sleep!

Language focus extra

Present perfect for indefinite past time

1 Write the past participle form of these irregular verbs. Then write the infinitive form of the irregular past participles.

1 speak _spoken_
2 be _____
3 take _____
4 see _____
5 come _____
6 feel _____
7 meet _____
8 write _____
9 gone _go_
10 done _____
11 sung _____
12 got _____
13 made _____
14 given _____
15 won _____
16 eaten _____

2 Complete the sentences. Use the present perfect form of the verbs in brackets.

1 _I've finished_ washing the car. (finish)
2 We _____ a window because it is really hot today. (open)
3 Your birthday card from Uncle David _____. (not arrive)
4 You _____ the shopping into the kitchen. (not carry)
5 They _____ visiting the museums and art galleries this weekend. (enjoy)
6 She _____ Leo four times this week. (email)
7 You _____ very well. You've got 10 points. (do)
8 He _____ the most beautiful portrait. Come and see it. (paint)

3 Circle the correct options.

1 My mum's not here. She's **gone** / **been** to the shops.
2 I've never **gone** / **been** to this gallery before. It's amazing.
3 He's **gone** / **been** on stage many times. He loves acting.
4 Keely's **gone** / **been** to Spain. I hope the weather's nice while she's there.
5 I've **gone** / **been** shopping on this street before.
6 They've **gone** / **been** cycling. They'll be back soon.

Present perfect – questions

4 Look at the table. Write present perfect questions with *ever* and the correct answers. ✓ = yes and ✗ = no.

	Charlotte	Aiden and Milo	You
Climb a mountain	¹✓	³✗	⁵?
Win a prize	²✗	⁴✓	⁶?

1 _Has Charlotte ever climbed a mountain?_
  Yes, she has.
2 _____
3 _____
4 _____
5 _____
6 _____

5 Complete the questions with the correct form of the present perfect. Then match the questions with the answers.

1 _Have you ever made_ (you / ever / make) dinner for your family? _c_
2 _____ (you / ever / do) karaoke? ___
3 How many different countries _____ (you / go) to? ___
4 _____ (your grandmother / ever / send) you an email? ___
5 Where _____ (your brothers / go)? ___
6 Which of these DVDs _____ (you / see)? ___

a Just three. Ireland, France and Japan.
b They've gone camping for the weekend.
c Yes, I have. I love cooking.
d No, I haven't. I don't like singing in front of people.
e I haven't seen any of them, I think.
f Yes, she has. She's really good at using computers.

98 Language Focus Extra

Language focus extra

Present perfect with still, yet, already and just

1 Complete the sentences with still, yet, already or just.
1. You ____still____ haven't bought me a birthday present.
2. I haven't seen the new Superman film _____ .
3. I've _____ tidied my room, so don't touch anything!
4. Harry's _____ broken his new computer. He's only had it for two weeks!
5. They haven't asked their parents for permission _____ .
6. Sorry, but I've _____ made plans for this weekend.
7. I've _____ found out that we're going skiing next month! I'm so excited!
8. Lucy _____ hasn't decided what she wants to do at university.

2 Put the words in the correct order to make sentences.
1. already / the news / have / I / heard
   I have already heard the news.
2. tidied / yet / you / Have / your bedroom / ?
   _____
3. me / hasn't / She / phoned / still
   _____
4. just / hungry / I'm / dinner / I've / not / because / had
   _____
5. home / already / He / has / gone
   _____
6. arrived / still / haven't / They
   _____
7. heard / amazing / just / I've / busker / an
   _____
8. yet / he / the book / read / Has / ?
   _____

Present perfect with for and since

3 Complete the table with the words in the box.

| three weeks   Monday   2008   Christmas |
| a long time   two hours |

for	since
three weeks	

4 Circle the correct options.
1. I've had my mobile **для** / since a year.
2. We've been here **for** / **since** this morning.
3. She hasn't spoken to me **for** / **since** months.
4. It hasn't rained **for** / **since** April.
5. Laura's been my friend **for** / **since** we were six.
6. They haven't seen each other **for** / **since** twelve weeks.

Present perfect and past simple

5 Circle the correct options.
1. ___ out with your friends last weekend?
   a Have you gone   **b Did you go**
2. I ___ when we went to the beach.
   a 've been happy   b was happy
3. ___ in Spain all your life?
   a Have you lived   b Did you live
4. Eric ___ golf before.
   a has never played   b never played
5. She still ___ the monkeys.
   a hasn't seen   b didn't see
6. I ___ you like painting.
   a haven't known   b didn't know

6 Complete the conversation. Use the present perfect or the past simple form of the verbs in brackets.

Mum:	Sam, ¹ *Have you seen* (you see) Julia?
Sam:	No, I ² _____ (see) her since last night. We ³ _____ (watch) TV when she came home. She was tired, so she ⁴ _____ (go) to bed early. Why?
Mum:	She isn't here, and she ⁵ _____ (not go) to school. Her teacher ⁶ _____ (just call).
Sam:	I don't know. ⁷ _____ (you ask) Dad?
Mum:	I rang the office, but he ⁸ _____ (still not reply) to my message.
Julia:	Hi!
Mum:	Julia! Where ⁹ _____ (you be)?
Julia:	Sorry, Mum. I ¹⁰ _____ (take) the bus to school but I ¹¹ _____ (come back) because I ¹² _____ (not feel) very well. I ¹³ _____ (just/take) some medicine.
Mum:	¹⁴ _____ (you have) breakfast yet?
Julia:	Yes, I have. I'm going back to bed.

Irregular verbs

infinitive	past simple	past participle
be	was/were	been
become	became	become
begin	began	begun
break	broke	broken
build	built	built
buy	bought	bought
catch	caught	caught
choose	chose	chosen
come	came	come
do	did	done
drink	drank	drunk
drive	drove	driven
eat	ate	eaten
fall	fell	fallen
feed	fed	fed
feel	felt	felt
find	found	found
fly	flew	flown
get	got	got
give	gave	given
go	went	gone
have	had	had
hear	heard	heard
keep	kept	kept
know	knew	known
learn	learnt/learned	learnt/learned
leave	left	left
lose	lost	lost
make	made	made
meet	met	met
pay	paid	paid
put	put	put
read	read	read
run	ran	run
say	said	said
see	saw	seen
send	sent	sent
sit	sat	sat
sleep	slept	slept
speak	spoke	spoken
spend	spent	spent
swim	swam	swum
take	took	taken
teach	taught	taught
tell	told	told
think	thought	thought
wear	wore	worn
win	won	won
write	wrote	written

Phonemic symbols

consonants

/p/	pencil
/b/	bag
/t/	town
/d/	day
/tʃ/	cheese
/dʒ/	juice
/k/	cake
/g/	get
/f/	food
/v/	very
/θ/	Thursday
/ð/	that
/s/	speak
/z/	zebra
/ʃ/	shoe
/ʒ/	usually
/m/	mum
/n/	name
/ŋ/	sing
/h/	house
/l/	like
/r/	red
/w/	water
/j/	you

vowels

/i:/	see
/ɪ/	sit
/ʊ/	book
/u:/	zoo
/e/	pen
/ə/	teacher
/ɜ:/	bird
/ɔ:/	boring
/æ/	that
/ʌ/	run
/ɑ:/	car
/ɒ/	lost

diphthongs

/eɪ/	say
/ɪə/	hear
/ʊə/	pure
/ɔɪ/	enjoy
/əʊ/	know
/eə/	chair
/aɪ/	buy
/aʊ/	now

Thanks and acknowledgments

The authors and publishers would like to thank a number of people whose support has proved invaluable during the planning, writing and production process of this course.

We would like to thank Diane Nicholls for researching and writing the Get it Right pages, Alice Martin for writing the original Starter Unit, Ingrid Wisniewska for writing the original Review sections and Mick Green for writing the original Grammar Extra sections.

The authors and publishers are grateful to the following contributors:
Blooberry: concept design
emc design Limited: text design and layout
emc design Limited: cover design
David Morritt and Ian Harker – DSound: audio recordings
Ruth Cox: editing

Development of this publication has made use of the Cambridge English Corpus (CEC). The CEC is a computer database of contemporary spoken and written English, which currently stands at over one billion words. It includes British English, American English and other varieties of English. It also includes the Cambridge Learner Corpus, developed in collaboration with the University of Cambridge ESOL Examinations. Cambridge University Press has built up the CEC to provide evidence about language use that helps to produce better language teaching materials.

The authors and publishers acknowledge the following sources of copyright material and are grateful for the permissions granted. While every effort has been made, it has not always been possible to identify the sources of all the material used, or to trace all copyright holders. If any omissions are brought to our notice, we will be happy to include the appropriate acknowledgements on reprinting.

p. 5 (BL): Corbis/Clifford White; p. 6 (B): Alamy/©Picture Partners; p. 8 (TR): age fotostock/stefano gulmanelli; p. 9 (TR): Getty Images/David Trood; p. 10 (CL): Alamy/©Patrick Eden; p. 11 (BL): Shutterstock Images/Benjamin Simeneta; p. 12 (C): Shutterstock Images/A.Hornung; p. 12 (B): Alamy/©PhotoAlto; p. 15 (BR): Alamy/©MBI; p. 17 (CR): Getty Images/Claudia Dewald; p. 20 (C): Shutterstock Images/Anchiy; p. 21 (BL): Alamy/©Terry Foster; p. 21 (C): Alamy/©My Lit'l Eye; p. 22 (BL): Shutterstock Images/Alexander Raths; p. 25 (TR): Shutterstock Images/lzf; p. 28 (BR): REX/Nils Jorgensen; p. 29 (CR): Alamy/©Roberto Herrett; p. 30 (BR): Alamy/©Scott Hortop Images; p. 31 (BL): Alamy/©Marek Stepan; p. 32 (B): Corbis/Paul Hackett; p. 37 (BR): Alamy/©Cate Brown; p. 38 (TR): Alamy/©Art Directors & TRIP; p. 39 (TL): Shutterstock Images/Monkey Business Images; p. 39 (BR): Shutterstock Images/Mitotico; p. 40 (TL): Shutterstock Images/Roland Zihlmann; p. 41 (TC): Shutterstock Images/ilovezion; p. 41 (TR): Shutterstock Images/Ammit Jack; p. 41 (BL): Shutterstock Images/Anton_Ivanov; p. 42 (CL): Shutterstock Images/NAN728; p. 42 (BL): Getty Images/Rolf Bruderer; p. 47 (TR): Getty Images/Zero Creatives; p. 48 (CL): Shutterstock Images/ARENA Creative; p. 49 (TL): Alamy/©Design Pics Inc.; p. 49 (BR): Getty Images/monkeybusinessimages; p. 50 (BL): Alamy/©Picture Partners; p. 51 (TL): Shutterstock Images/Monkey Business Images; p. 52 (TR): Shutterstock Images/MJTH; p. 54 (CL): Shutterstock Images/wallybird; p. 58 (CR): Alamy/©Westend61 GmbH; p. 60 (TR): Shutterstock Images/Refat; p. 61 (BL): Alamy/©Angela Hampton Picture Library; p. 62 (B): Alamy/©Emiliano Joanes; p. 68 (CL): Alamy/©Jenny Matthews; p. 69 (TL): Shutterstock Images/Olimpik; p. 69 (BR): Shutterstock Images/Photographee.eu; p. 71 (BL): Shutterstock Images/Monkey Business Images; p. 72 (C): Alamy/©imageBROKER; p. 74 (TL): Shutterstock Images/sonya etchison; p. 78 (BL): Alamy/©Jim West; p. 78 (TR): Shutterstock Images/Bakalusha; p. 80 (TR): Alamy/©Islandstock; p. 81 (TL): Shutterstock Images/bikeriderlondon; p. 81 (BL): Alamy/©Michael Klinec; p. 82 (BL): Getty Images/Jupiterimages; p. 84 (TR): Alamy/©Andrew Butterton; p. 88 (B): Alamy/©Caroline Commins; p. 89 (BL): Shutterstock Images/Nagy-Bagoly Arpad; p. 90 (CR): Shutterstock Images/Prudkov; p. 91 (CR): Alamy/©Keith Pritchard/ARGO Images.

Front cover photograph by Getty Images/Eduardo Garcia.

The publishers are grateful to the following illustrators:

David Belmonte p. 19, 27; Russ Cook p. 3 (TL), 35, 65, 75; Nigel Dobbyn p. 14, 57, 77; Mark Draisey p. 7, 59, 68, 70; Mark Duffin p. 9, 29, 79; Andrew Painter p. 18; Martin Sanders p. 3 (R), 55; Tony Wilkins p. 20, 47.

All video stills by kind permission of Discovery Communications, LLC 2015.

CAMBRIDGE
UNIVERSITY PRESS

University Printing House, Cambridge CB2 8BS, United Kingdom

One Liberty Plaza, 20th Floor, New York, NY 10006, USA

477 Williamstown Road, Port Melbourne, VIC 3207, Australia

314–321, 3rd Floor, Plot 3, Splendor Forum, Jasola District Centre, New Delhi – 110025, India

103 Penang Road, #05-06/07, Visioncrest Commercial, Singapore 238467

Cambridge University Press is part of the University of Cambridge.

It furthers the University's mission by disseminating knowledge in the pursuit of education, learning and research at the highest international levels of excellence.

www.cambridge.org
Information on this title: www.cambridge.org/9781107489387

© Cambridge University Press 2015

This publication is in copyright. Subject to statutory exception and to the provisions of relevant collective licensing agreements, no reproduction of any part may take place without the written permission of Cambridge University Press.

First published 2015

20 19 18 17 16

Printed in Great Britain by CPI Group (UK) Ltd, Croydon CR0 4YY

A catalogue record for this publication is available from the British Library

ISBN 978-1-107-46764-4 Student's Book with Online Workbook and Online Practice
ISBN 978-1-107-46762-0 Student's Book
ISBN 978-1-107-46773-6 Workbook with Online Practice
ISBN 978-1-107-48938-7 Combo A with Online Workbook and Online Practice
ISBN 978-1-107-48940-0 Combo B with Online Workbook and Online Practice
ISBN 978-1-107-46775-0 Teacher's Book
ISBN 978-1-107-46776-7 Audio CDs (3)
ISBN 978-1-107-46779-8 Video DVD
ISBN 978-1-107-48942-4 Presentation Plus DVD-ROM

Additional resources for this publication at www.cambridgelms.org/eyesopen

Cambridge University Press has no responsibility for the persistence or accuracy of URLs for external or third-party internet websites referred to in this publication, and does not guarantee that any content on such websites is, or will remain, accurate or appropriate. Information regarding prices, travel timetables, and other factual information given in this work is correct at the time of first printing but Cambridge University Press does not guarantee the accuracy of such information thereafter.